Competency-Based Interviews

Master the Tough New Interview Style and Give Them the Answers That Will Win You the Job

By

Robin Kessler

CAREER
PRESS
Franklin Lakes, NJ

COMPETENCY-BASED INTERVIEWS
EDITED BY JODI BRANDON
TYPESET BY ASTRID DERIDDER
Cover design by DesignConcept
Printed in the U.S.A. by Book-mart Press
Cartoons found on pages 72, 84, 98, 114, 144, 176, 198, and 212 by Steven Lait, 2006.

To order this title, please call toll-free 1-800-CAREER-1 (NJ and Canada: 201-848-0310) to order using VISA or MasterCard, or for further information on books from Career Press.

The Career Press, Inc., 3 Tice Road, PO Box 687, Franklin Lakes, NJ 07417
www.careerpress.com

Library of Congress Cataloging-in-Publication Data available upon request.

Dedication

This is for my mother, with love and thanks.

Acknowledgments

As always, a huge thank you to everyone who helped with this book. I would, however, like to give a few people some special recognition.

To Paula Hanson, thank you for doing the initial editing and providing advice when I came up against problems. Any kind of problems. And for hanging in as a good friend for a very long time.

To Steven Lait, editorial cartoonist for the Oakland Tribune and ANG Group, who drew the cartoons for this book, thank you for doing great work for Competency-Based Interviews, and being the best editorial cartoonist on the planet and one of my favorite cousins.

To the consultants, Cara Capretta Raymond, Michael Friedman, Dr. Kay Lillig Cotter, and Ken Abosch, thank you for sharing your expertise, time, opinions, and personal competencies. Having the opportunity to talk with each of you has helped me make this book considerably stronger.

To David Heath, Dessie Nash, Blake Nolingberg, Mindy Wertheimer, Erica Graham, Chip Smith, Kalen Phillips, Stephen Sye, Diane Schad Dayhoff, Mary Alice Eureste, and Bill Baumgardt, thank you for being subject matter experts in your professional areas and answering all my questions.

To Dr. Jon Wiener and Martha Williams, thank you for sharing some of your favorite quotations with me.

To Ron Fry, Michael Pye, Kristen Parkes, Linda Rienecker, Laurie Kelly-Pye, Jodi Brandon, Astrid deRidder, and the rest of the staff at Career Press, thank you for doing a great job of making my words look good, the book look better, and being great to work with.

To my other friends and relatives, thank you for putting up with my leaving early, not calling as often, and not being as available to go out to dinner, the movies, or anything else. Since this book is now finished, call me.

—Robin Kessler

Contents

Introduction

What can you do today to be a star at interviewing and improve your career? How can you get that specific offer you want from the organization you want to work for? How can you move forward in your career?

Think strategically.

What makes Lance Armstrong keep winning the Tour de France? It takes more than luck to win a major sports event seven times. He's been so successful that, as of 2005, he's chosen to retire.

Why do publishers choose certain book proposals and not others? Why do certain products do especially well and others don't?

How did Oprah become a star, and what does she do to make sure she stays a star? How can she be so good at interviewing others on her show, acting, and developing and publishing her magazine? When Oprah decides to promote a book through her book club or by having the author on her show, book sales increase dramatically.

Why did you—or someone you know—get into a prestigious college? Why do certain people get selected for the best assignments and the best jobs? What causes other qualified candidates to be rejected?

The answers to these questions are complex, but if we really think about it, there are three basic steps we all need to take to improve our ability to get what we want.

What It Takes to Win

1. Learning what it takes to win is the first step.
2. Doing the things that it takes to win is the second step.
3. Recognizing that what it takes to win changes— sometimes rapidly—is the third step.

The faster we identify the changes and adjust our own approach, the faster we will be successful. Realistically, we need to expect these changes. New tools, new approaches, and new strategies can cause decision-makers to make different decisions. If we adapt to these changes earlier than others, we increase our probability of winning.

That's it. Lance and Oprah may have extra-strong athletic or artistic abilities, and they are obviously smarter than average. But both have also overcome major life challenges, namely cancer and child abuse. Clearly, both celebrities figured out what it took to get ahead in their fields, and they have mastered staying ahead of the game as their competition became more savvy.

One of the key characteristics that will significantly help you manage your own career as effectively as possible is learning how to interview more effectively and convince the interviewer that you are the best candidate for the job. Interviewing well is critical if you want to be successful.

So how can we take the three steps that it takes to win and apply them to interviewing? This book will show you how to be more successful by:

- Teaching you how to recognize the changes in interviewing at the most sophisticated organizations.

- Explaining what today's interviewers are looking for.

- Helping you adjust your own way of interviewing to emphasize how your competencies match the employer's needs.

- Developing a plan to ensure you perform well in every critical interview.

When systems change and grow, we need to be smarter than our competitors and recognize those changes as early as possible, the way Lance and Oprah have always done. If we aren't aware, our own careers may be affected in a negative way. We need time to develop and adjust our strategy, because employers do periodically change the systems they use to select employees.

If we don't change our own approach, we will eventually become less valuable to our employer. We all need to take responsibility for actively managing our careers, and that includes changing our strategy to respond to the changes introduced by employers. As we become even more astute, we may be able to anticipate some of these changes and prepare for them.

This book will give you a new—and better—strategy you can use to help you interview more effectively and improve your ability to get the job you want in the best organizations. If you use this approach, you will increase your chances of:

- Being selected for the most competitive positions.

- Winning the best job at a new organization.

- Getting a great first job or internship.

- Being chosen for that critical promotion in your current organization.

- Taking control of your career path.

- Increasing your salary.

- Getting more satisfying assignments and more challenging work.

What's Different?

Understanding the way human resources managers, line managers, and professionals approach selecting employees has always given candidates an advantage in the interview process. If you know what the interviewer is looking for—and you are savvy enough to know how to use this information—you will have an edge in the interview.

I've been told that at least half of the Fortune 500 and other major organizations in the United States, in Europe, and internationally are now using competency-based systems to help select and manage their human resources.[1] Here are just a few examples: American Express, Johnson & Johnson, Coca-Cola, Toyota, Bank of America, BP, Wells Fargo, General Motors, HP, Radio Shack, HCA, Carlson Companies, BHP, IBM, General Electric, PDVSA, Anheuser-Busch, Girl Scouts USA, the U.S. Federal Reserve System, and the province of British Columbia in Canada.

Some of these organizations have worked with competency-based systems for more than 15 years, and they are becoming increasingly sophisticated with the applications they are using. Other companies, government agencies, and nonprofit organizations have adopted competencies more recently, or are looking at the possibility of using them in the near future. Competency-based applications help organizations manage their human resources—from selecting employees to evaluating, training, paying, and promoting them.

Competency-based selection processes and **competency-based appraisals** are the two most common ways companies are using competencies to help improve the caliber of their employees. More and more companies are including a list of competencies they need in their own Website ads and Internet advertisements on Websites such as *www.monster.com* and *www.careerbuilder.com*. Since January 2003, when I saw the need for the book *Competency-Based Resumes*, the number of jobsite advertisements that specifically list the competencies the employer is looking for continues to significantly increase every time I check.

On November 23, 2005, Monster.com ran advertisements asking for competencies from organizations of all sizes. Companies with competency-based job advertisements that day included:

- Kaiser Permanente
- Ernst & Young
- Marsh & McLennan
- International Paper
- Hitachi Consulting
- Heidrick & Struggles
- Royal Caribbean Cruises

- Deloitte
- Shell Oil
- Ingersoll Rand
- St. Paul Travelers
- MetLife
- Honeywell

That same day, CareerBuilder.com ran an advertisement for a Competency Modeling Manager for Wal-Mart. Rockwell Automation advertised for an Engineering Competency Leader, and Excellus BlueCross BlueShield in Rochester, New York, was looking for a Manager, Project Manager Competency Center. McGraw-Hill advertised for a Director, Talent Management who would "conduct a needs analysis to create an executive competency model and 'future' leader profile." Other organizations running ads on CareerBuilder.com specifically mentioned competencies on November 23, 2005, included:

- Sears
- Administrative Office of the United States Courts
- PriceWaterhouseCoopers
- Cingular Wireless

Employees at the best competency-based employers have the ability to look up information about critical competencies on their employer's Website or in employee handbooks or manuals. The competencies for their current positions are almost always covered as part of their appraisal.

What Are Competencies?

Paul Green, in his book *Building Robust Competencies* (Jossey-Bass, 1999), defines an individual competency as "a written description of measurable work habits and personal skills used to achieve a work objective." Some organizations use a slightly different definition for competencies: underlying characteristics, behavior, knowledge, and skills required to differentiate performance. They define what superior performers do more often, in more situations, and with better results.

Put simply, competencies are the key characteristics that the most successful performers have that help them be so successful. Organizations benefit from working with competencies because it gives them a better, more sophisticated way to manage, measure, and improve the quality of their employees.

The use of competencies is continuing to grow. According to Signe Spencer, a senior consultant with the Hay Group in Boston and the coauthor of *Competence at Work* (John Wiley & Sons, 1993), "In the last ten years, we have seen an explosion of interest in competency work at all levels worldwide."

The relevant competencies that have been identified for all positions organization-wide are called **core competencies**. But competencies used in interviewing (and other applications) may be identified at the department or functional level, or even at the individual level. It takes different competencies to be successful as an accountant than to be successful as a sales professional. In Chapter 2, I will spend more time explaining competencies and giving you the information you need to successfully identify the relevant competencies for the position you want, before the interview.

Many organizations choose not to use the term *competencies*. They call the *key characteristics that it takes to be successful* by other terms: success factors, attributes, values, dimensions, and so on. There are subtle differences in what each of these terms mean, and decision-makers have good reasons for choosing them. For candidates, though, it simply makes sense to look at all of these categories for information describing what the employer is really looking for—those key characteristics or competencies.

Competencies are not just a trend, and the competency-based systems designed by consultants and corporations can be complex. This book will help you understand competency-based selection systems and give you the tools you need, as a candidate, to navigate your way through them.

What Are Competency-Based Interviews?

Today, more interviewers at the best employers are using behavioral interviewing techniques to help determine how competent candidates are in the key areas most critical for success. Behavioral interviewing has been used for more than 20 years in most sophisticated organizations, but many of these organizations have only been using behavioral interview questions *targeting relevant competencies* in the last five or 10 years. Other organizations began working with competency-based interviewing even before that timeframe.

Interviewers at many of the best organizations are being trained to use competency-based systems and evaluate candidates in a much more complex way than in the past. They are taught to:

- Evaluate the candidate's fit for the position based on their perceived competency level.

- Assess the candidate's nonverbal and verbal communication in a more sophisticated way.

Organizations may use different names, including targeted selection interviewing and evidence-based interviewing, to describe what is essentially competency-based interviewing. Some competency-based interviewing is based on the approach of asking primary questions targeting each key competency. Another approach asks interviewers to identify evidence of competencies by listening closely to the answers to questions, follow-up questions (also called probes), and more follow-up questions. In Chapter 1, we'll be looking at these approaches in more detail.

Most career counselors and candidates haven't changed their approach to interviewing, resumes, and other job search techniques to consider the competencies more of the best employers are now looking for. Instead, they are marketing candidate strengths and accomplishments the same way they always have. It is time to accept that the job market has changed and become more sophisticated. It simply makes sense to change your own approach.

Competencies are the way the majority of the most respected organizations measure whether to interview and hire candidates. For candidates or employees trying to turn their interview into a job offer, it's time to change and be more strategic. It's time to understand how to use your own competencies to convince employers you are the best candidate for them—because you can prove to them you have the critical competencies they need.

> *As the saying goes, you don't want to be fighting today's war using equipment, strategy, and tactics from the last century.*

It's up to you to learn how to interview the current, competency-based way. To do this, you need to:

1. Understand competency-based interview systems.

2. Identify the key competencies for the position.

3. Know what interviewers are trained to look for.

4. Expect competency-based behavioral questions.

5. Prove your competencies with examples.

6. Look like a strong candidate.

7. Consider other important interview tips.

8. Check to make sure you are ready for the interview.

9. Look at case studies for ideas to make your interviewing stronger.

10. Understand how a typical competency-based interview flows.

11. Learn from other interviewees.

12. Send a thank-you note, follow up, get the offer, and negotiate.

Once you have started your new position, you may also need to learn to conduct competency-based interviews. And you will be more successful in your new position if you take the time to follow the suggestions we give in Chapter 13 on managing your career in a competency-based organization and in the final chapter on how to think long-term and make change work for you.

By following the suggestions in the book, you will perform better in any interview and increase the probability of an offer. Learning to master the competency-based interview will give you skills that will help you interact better with other professionals in meetings, one-on-one interactions, and other types of interviews.

Organizations also benefit from their candidates learning how to be interviewed more effectively. If more people give good, thoughtful answers that illustrate their experience with competencies, managers will have better, more complete information to use when they make their decision about which candidate is the most competent for the job.

Many strong, highly competent candidates may benefit from interview coaching or training to help them think about their *best* accomplishments in each competency area before the interview.

Most managers know that the best employees aren't always the best interviewees.

Are you ready to start sharpening your interviewing skills so the interviewer will realize you are the most competent candidate? Let's start now.

At the end of every chapter, a question and answer summary is included for your review. These summaries will give you the opportunity to reread the most important points and ensure you understand them. Take the time you need to grasp the concepts and ideas before moving on to the next chapter.

Key Points for the Introduction

"An *individual competency* is a written description of measurable work habits and personal skills used to achieve a work objective."

–Paul Green

Key Questions	Answers
What does it take to win in today's organizations?	1. Learning what it takes to win. 2. Doing the things that it takes to win. 3. Recognizing that what it takes to win changes—sometimes rapidly.
What are competencies?	The key characteristics that the most successful employees have that help them be so successful.
What are core competencies?	Core competencies are skills used organization-wide to help achieve organization objectives or goals.

Key Questions	Answers
How can you increase your ability to get the position you want?	*Competency-based organizations rely on a different system for looking at what it takes to be successful in jobs, particularly when selecting, promoting, and training their employees. Understanding how competency-based systems work is vital to success in today's organizations.*
	Surprise! The most important thing to remember is that these systems always change. You need to adjust your own approach to match the employer's changes.
In addition to the core competencies, what are the other levels of competencies?	• Department or functional • Individual
What are the two most common competency-based applications?	• Competency-based appraisals • Competency-based screening and interviewing to select candidates.
What are behavioral interview questions?	Behavioral interviewing is based on the theory that past behavior is the best predictor of future behavior. In other words, *past success predicts future success.*

Key Questions	Answers
What can you do to excel in interviews for very competitive positions?	To master the tough interview style, your answers to interview questions must be focused (focused on the competencies desired), powerful (use powerful words to describe your competency), and concise (make a point, make it clear, and use precise wording).
How can you keep promoting your competencies?	It is important to keep marketing your competencies even after getting the position. Other strategic marketing tools are: competency-based resumes, cover letters, networking, and interview skills. Remember to focus on the competencies required by your prospective employer—or your current employer, if you want to be considered for promotion or other opportunities.
How are companies using competencies to strengthen their workforce?	They are using competencies to: <ul><li>Advertise for candidates</li><li>Screen candidate resumes</li><li>Interview using behavioral techniques</li><li>Select employees</li><li>Evaluate employees</li><li>Train employees</li><li>Promote employees</li><li>Reward employees</li><li>Determine assignments</li></ul>

Chapter 1

Understand Competency-Based Interview Systems

When we were students, most of us realized the importance of understanding what the teacher or professor was looking for—which assignments were required and which were optional. And if we are playing sports, we need to understand the strengths, vulnerabilities, and game plan of our opponent, even if we are the #1 seed in the tournament. When we give a business presentation, we need to identify our goals and understand the needs and interests of the audience before we start developing the speech.

Figuring out what other people are looking for is critical to being successful in most things throughout life. Assuming we have the basics, we simply have to provide the evidence and, in an interview, convince them that we *fit*.

Before we start preparing for an interview, it is important to understand the method of interviewing that will be used by the interviewer. Some organizations are still traditional in their approaches to interviewing. Many managers still ask questions that help them make decisions about candidates based simply on whether or not they *like* them. In addition, they may focus on whether the candidate meets their basic requirement on credentials, such as grades and class standing. Most law firms and many of the more traditional companies are still interviewing candidates this way.

Some managers use hypothetical questions based on giving the candidate a scenario and asking what he or she would do. People who like this interview style believe it gives them a chance to see how candidates think on their feet, but many others believe that it is not as effective as finding out how individuals have performed in the past.

Most of the managers at organizations with strong, positive reputations have realized that the old-style interviews don't seem to be that effective in helping them choose employees. They've changed to the competency-based interview style.

What's Changed?

Recognizing how the labor market has changed—and learning how to make those changes work for you—can make the difference between success and failure.

The most sophisticated employers are primarily using competency-based interview systems to select candidates. If you haven't interviewed recently or if you come from a different culture, you probably know you need some help to do well in the interview. Some candidates think they know what to expect in the interview, and it may take a few bad experiences before they decide their old approach is not working as well as it used to.

But even if you are articulate, think well on your feet, have the best credentials, and are confident you are a great candidate, preparing for the interview is important. Remember that how well you perform on the interview gives the interviewers an idea of the quality of work they can expect from you in the future.

Whether you are writing a resume, preparing for an interview, or getting ready for a performance evaluation, becoming more aware of what competencies the employer is looking for is the first step to help make you more successful. The next step? Learn what you need to know to prove to the employer that you are strong in these critical competency areas.

How Does a Competency-Based Interview Work?

Very simply, a competency-based interview uses behavioral questions to help the interviewer assess the candidate based on critical competencies that have been identified by the employer. The interview is highly structured, with key questions provided for the interviewers to help them determine how strong candidates are in specific competency areas.

Key Definition

Competency-based interviews are structured and use behavioral questions to help the interviewer assess candidates based on critical competencies identified for the position.

Whether you are a candidate who wants to work for an organization using competency-based systems or an employee currently working in a competency-based company, it is important to recognize that it may be time to change your own approach to the process. Retool and retrain. Adjust the sails. Add a warm-up period before running. Accept the fact: In today's most sophisticated organizations, almost all are using competency-based interviews.

The most commonly used competency-based interviewing style is based upon asking candidates primary questions targeted to the critical competencies for the position. Almost every major consulting firm working to help organizations identify competencies, including Lominger, Personnel Decisions, Inc., Hay Group, and Hewitt Associates, encourages its clients to use structured, competency-based interviewing processes that they have developed.

One well-known example of this approach is *Targeted Selection Interviewing*, which was developed by the consulting firm Development Dimensions Inc. On its Website, the firm markets *Targeted Selection* by saying it uses behavioral interviewing and helps organizations:

- Identify the competencies needed for all key positions.

- Build interviewing skills and confidence for more accurate selection decisions.

- Increase the efficiency and effectiveness of the employee selection process.

Another interviewing approach related to competency-based interviews starts with the manager asking a question about a major accomplishment and then asking follow-up questions to probe for additional information about competencies, strengths, and weaknesses. An example of this approach is Lou Adler's *The One Question Interview*.

Both styles are covered in more detail later in this chapter.

Although the style may be a little different, managers are taught to ask candidates behavioral questions, based on the theory that past behavior is the best predictor of future behavior. In other words, past success is the best predictor of future success. The managers are then asked to assess how *competent* the candidate is in several critical areas.

Key Definition

Behavioral questions are based on the theory that past behavior is the best predictor of future behavior.

To gain the understanding we really need to perform well in a competency-based interview, we need to first understand the answers to this question: What are the two basic interview styles that consider competencies?

Interview Style #1:
Competency-Based Interviews (Most Typical Approach) Example: Johnson & Johnson

Johnson & Johnson, ranked #1 on the 2005 Corporate Reputation Survey[1], has worked with competency-based interviewing for more than 10 years. They have developed interview guides for their senior leaders (executives), people and individual leaders (professionals and managers), and for campus interviewing.

Susan Millard, Vice President for Strategic Talent Management at Johnson & Johnson, said, "Predicting future success on the job and the competencies that matter the most to performance, and operating with the highest ethical standards are critical to assure we have the talent needed to power our growth and culture at J&J." She also talked about how successful their 2005 recruiting event with 700 MBAs and managers was because they used their updated competency-based Global Leadership Profile Interview Guides and were able to identify some particularly strong candidates.

Their interview guides review how the interviewer should prepare before the interview, suggest ways to open the interview, encourage the interviewer to review the candidate's background and ask questions, and provide several behavioral questions for each critical competency for the position that interviewers can choose from during the interview. The interviewer is asked to rate the candidate on the competency and his or her communication skills.

Though every example in J&J's guide is strong, I chose to show you the "Results and Performance Driven" example, because it represents one of the most frequently used competencies—by every organization. Other organizations often use synonyms to describe the same competency. This one competency can be called:

- Achieves Results

- Drive for Results

- Performance Bias

- Achieves Goals

(For explanations of the ratings for the following chart, see Chapter 3.)

Results and Performance Driven	Key Examples
Goal oriented; remains persistent when obstacles are encountered; encourages others to be accountable for their actions; relentlessly focused and committed to customer service; thinks creatively.	☐ **Flawless execution**—Holds self, direct reports, and others accountable for seamless and compliant execution of tasks and projects. ☐ **Accepts stretch goals**—Eagerly embraces stretch goals; measures achievements through metrics. ☐ **Customer centric thinking**—Makes the customer the center for all decisions to build value; imposes customer focus on others and challenges them to exceed customer expectations.

Planned Behavioral Questions

1. Describe an instance when you were particularly effective at achieving end results. What steps did you take to achieve these results?
2. Think of an example when you consistently exceeded internal or external customer expectations. How did you do this? What approach did you use?
3. Provide an example of a project or team you managed in which there were many obstacles to overcome. What did you do to address those obstacles?
4. Tell me about an example of what you have done to obtain information to better understand a customer. What did you do? How did this information improve your customer service?
5. It is not always easy to achieve required work goals or objectives. Describe a stretch goal or objective that you were able to achieve. Why was this a stretch goal? What was the result?

Situation/Task	Action	Result

Communication

Results and Performance Driven Rating

Reprinted with permission of Johnson & Johnson Strategic Talent Management

Interview Style #2:
The 1-Question Interview

Another current approach to interviewing starts with one question and asks the candidate a series of follow-up questions to probe for additional information. This interview technique provides an interesting and different way to assess a candidate by listening for evidence of the candidate's competency (and critical competencies) in his answers to the questions.

The basic technique is shown in this excerpt from an article by consultant Lou Adler, whose firm, Adler Concepts, teaches interviewing skills classes to some major clients. He encourages the interviewer to first ask the candidate to think about his or her most significant accomplishment, and then to tell the interviewer about it. Then he teaches the interviewers to probe and get the following information about the accomplishment from the candidate in 15 to 20 minutes:

- A complete description of the accomplishment.

- The company you worked for and what it did.

- The actual results achieved: numbers, facts, changes made, details, amounts.

- When it took place.

- How long it took.

- The importance of this accomplishment to the company.

- Your title and role.

- Why you were chosen.

- The three to four biggest challenges you faced and how you dealt with them.

- A few examples of leadership and initiative.

- Some of the major decisions made.

- The environment and resources available.

- How you made more resources available.

- The technical skills needed to accomplish the objective.

- The technical skills learned and how long it took to learn them.

- The actual role you played.

- The team involved and all of the reporting relationships.

- Some of the biggest mistakes you made.

- How you changed and grew as a person.

- What you would do differently if you could do it again.

- Aspects of the project you truly enjoyed.

- Aspects you didn't especially care about.

- The budget available and your role in preparing it and managing it.

- How you did on the project vs. the plan.

- How you developed the plan.

- How you motivated and influenced others, with specific examples to prove your claims.

- How you dealt with conflict with specific examples.

- Anything else you felt was important to the success of the project.

Adler encourages interviewers to conduct this type of interview because he believes "the insight gained from this type of question would be remarkable. Just about everything you need to know about a person's competency can be extracted from this type of question.'"

Comparing the 2 Types of Interviews That Consider Competencies

From your perspective, as an interviewee, what's the difference between the two types of interviews we've been talking about in this chapter?

Each type of interview gives the interviewers good, substantive information about candidates. Both ask the interviewers to listen to the candidate's answers and determine how strong they are in critical competency areas important to be successful in the position.

The most common type of competency-based interview looks at several of the most critical competencies and asks the candidate to answer behavioral questions targeting the competencies. The second type goes in depth on one or two accomplishments and asks the candidate to look at these accomplishments from different perspectives—including competencies.

So why does this matter? It is not as if the interviewer gives you a choice. And basically, you don't need to spend time worrying about the type of interview the interviewer is going to use.

But if you *do* recognize the type of interview, it may help you think ahead and give the interviewer slightly better answers.

By following the advice in this book, you'll be prepared for both types of interviews we've mentioned—and any variation of a competency-based interview that someone develops in the future. You need to start thinking about how to prepare for these types of interviews. This book, though, is going to emphasize helping you to prepare for the first type, because it is so much more common.

When you develop accomplishments proving you are strong in each relevant competency, you can expect follow-up questions to probe how much you know or simply to clarify something that is unclear to the interviewer. Start becoming aware of how each accomplishment can provide evidence in more than one competency area. As you think about each accomplishment, consider the follow-up questions you could be asked to get information about your competence in several key areas. If you do that, you will be ready for either type of interview.

Be smart, be savvy, and figure out what you can expect.

Key Points for Chapter 1	
Competency-based interviews are currently being used by many of the most sophisticated organizations throughout the world.	
Key Questions	**Answers**
Is every organization using competency-based interviewing methods?	Most of the more sophisticated organizations worldwide *are* using competency-based interviewing.
	But some of the more traditional companies and law firms are still interviewing and making important decisions based upon the candidate's credentials and if the interviewer likes the candidate.
How can you tell that you are being given a competency-based interview?	Competency-based interviews are highly structured and use behavioral questions to help the interviewer get good answers from the candidate. These answers help interviewers assess candidates more effectively based on the critical competencies identified for the position.

Key Questions	Answers
What is behavioral interviewing?	Interviewing based on the theory that past behavior is the best predictor of future behavior.
How are competency-based interviews highly structured?	Typically, most organizations have identified three to five primary questions targeting each critical competency area that interviewers may use to get the information from the candidate needed to assess their level of competence.
What is the difference between the two styles of interviewing mentioned in this chapter?	The first style is the most widely used type of competency-based interview. Interviewers will ask candidates behavioral questions targeting each competency area identified as being important to being successful in the position. Candidates have the opportunity to talk about a number of accomplishments. The second style asks the candidate to look at an accomplishment and then probe for additional information—including looking at accomplishments from the perspective of different competencies.

Chapter 2

Identify Key Competencies

I not only use all the brains that I have,
but all that I can borrow.
—Woodrow Wilson

Like former U.S. President Woodrow Wilson, many of us believe in trying to be as smart as we can before the actual interview. Taking the time to learn what the organization is looking for *before the interview* is critical if you plan to convince the interviewer that you are the best candidate for the job. If you need to borrow the information from other people or by doing online research, take the hint from Nike's advertisement: *Just do it.* Nike, by the way, is another company that works with competencies.

Countries sharing the same language can have different priorities for competencies, and within each country you can expect to have organizations with different needs—and different competencies. Organizations develop their own lists of competencies and may work closely with consultants to benefit from their expertise in competencies and competency modeling.

More conservative companies would probably emphasize different competencies than more progressive organizations, such as Ben and Jerry's or Starbucks. Think of the difference between United Airlines and Southwest, for example. Or IBM and Dell. In every case, the competencies need to be consistent with the corporate culture the senior managers are trying to create.

What is the best way to figure out what the hiring manager is going to be looking for in the interview? Competencies are a great place to start.

Some organizations have identified competencies for their positions, and they are listed as part of their online advertisements. The key competencies (or similar words such as *success factors, dimensions,* or *values*) may also be part of a job description that a recruiter can provide. Other organizations may not have directly listed their competencies for the position, but in reality, they are all looking for *competent people* for their positions—whether or not they have formally identified competencies.

For example, Coca-Cola listed an opportunity on Monster.com in December 2005 for a Human Resources Director in Atlanta, Georgia. In the advertisement, "General Competencies" were listed as:

Building Value-Based Relationships: Generating alliances internally and externally by continuously identifying and acting on those things that will create success for the Company and its customers, bottlers, suppliers, communities, and governments.

Contributing to Team Success: Actively participating as a committed member of a team and working with other team members to help complete goals and deliverables.

Customer Focus: Making customers (external and internal) and their needs a primary focus of one's actions; developing and sustaining productive customer relationships; creating and executing plans and solutions in collaboration with the customer.

Providing Feedback: Objectively observing, analyzing, and sharing your perception of other people's performance to reinforce or redirect behavior to improve performance and business results. Providing feedback that is timely, specific, behavioral, balanced, and constructive.

Work Standards: Setting high standards of performance for self; assuming responsibility and accountability for successfully completing assignments or tasks; self-imposing standards of excellence rather than having standards imposed.

Consulting: Providing timely, specific information, guidance, and recommendations to help groups, managers, and others make informed committed decisions that will lead to sustainable impact.

Establishing Collaborative Working Relationships: Developing and using collaborative relationships for the purpose of accomplishing work objectives; developing relationships with other individuals by listening, sharing ideas, and appreciating others' efforts.

When the competencies are not directly identified, you need to do several things to begin to identify the competencies for the position on your own—before the interview. The four major steps to identify the competencies are:

1. Think about the obvious competencies for the position.

2. Look at advertisements and postings from competitors.

3. Compile a list of competencies from other sources, including employment Websites, advertisements in newspapers, magazines and journals, professional associations, and the organization's Website.

4.   Select 10 to 15 competencies that would be the most critical for the position you are interested in from Appendix A.

If you already work for an organization and need to interview for a promotion or a new position, you may be able to find the relevant list of competencies for the position:

- On the company Website.

- On performance appraisals for employees currently in the position.

- In employee handbooks or other company manuals.

- By asking a colleague or friend working in the relevant department in the organization.

One of the main ways you can show how strong a candidate you are is to prepare—to do your homework. Take the initiative to be resourceful and make every effort to find this list. Even if the organization hasn't defined this list, you can make a smart and educated guess about the most critical competencies.

> *When the competencies aren't directly identified, look further.*

Step 1: Think About the Obvious Competencies for the Position

In sales, it is critical to focus on results. It doesn't matter how much the managers like you if you don't close the sale.

When you don't see the word *competencies* as a heading in an online job posting or advertisement, read further. You may see phrases and words that look like core, departmental, and individual competencies under headings such as "Required Qualifications," "Job Requirements," or "Required Knowledge, Skills, and Abilities."

Step 2: Look at Jobs Posted on the Websites of Organizations That Directly Compete With the Employer

Also check to see if any of the competitors have the equivalent position posted on Monster, CareerBuilder, or one of the other job sites on the Internet.

Then, try to decide if the same competencies fit the position you are interested in, or if they need to be reworked for any other reason. (In other words, consider the culture of the organization.) For example, it would be reasonable to assume that the corporate culture at Celestial Seasonings differs from the culture at Lipton Tea enough to cause the competencies that it takes to be successful to also be different—even for the equivalent position.

Step 3: Start to Compile a Complete, Thorough List of Competencies for Your Position

There are several ways to develop a broader list of competencies for a particular position. For example, if you are interested in being considered for an IT project manager's position at a company that has not listed competencies in its advertisement, go to:

● An employment Website, such as Monster.com or Dice.com, and type in "competencies IT project manager." Look through several of the ads to see if the competencies identified for these positions match what you know about the position at the particular organization you want to work for. (Remember that you do not have to limit *this* search to your geographic area!)

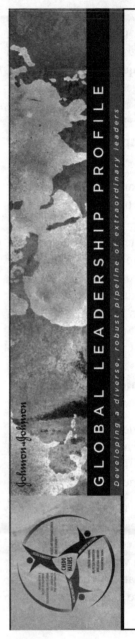

GLOBAL LEADERSHIP PROFILE

Developing a diverse, robust pipeline of extraordinary leaders

Johnson & Johnson

- Integrity and Credo-based Actions—lives Credo values; builds trust; tells the truth; initiates transparency into problems; demonstrates genuine caring for people

- Strategic Thinking—driven to envision a better future; takes any role or job and makes it better; has relentless dissatisfaction with status quo; motivated to leave things better than they were; a change agent

- Big Picture Orientation with Attention to Detail—able to cooperate in two "worlds" simultaneously e.g., growth and cost control, enterprise and operating company success; sees the why as well as the what; can zoom in or out as needed

- Organization and Talent Development—motivates and empowers others to achieve a desired action; enjoys developing a diverse group of people; champions diversity; instills confidence; attracts good people; demonstrates a track record of people development; brings out the best in others; net exporter of successful talent; invests time to be personally "connected" with the organization

- Intellectual Curiosity—sees the possibilities; willing to experiment; cultivates new ideas; comfortable with ambiguity and uncertainty

- Collaboration and Teaming—puts interest of enterprise about own; works well across functions and groups; builds teams effectively; inspires fellowship; instills a global mindset; champions best practices

- Sense of Urgency—proactively senses and responds to problems and opportunities; works to reduce "cycle" time; takes action when needed

- Prudent Risk-taking—inner confidence to take risks and learn from experience; courage to grab opportunities or shed non-viable businesses; willing to make tough calls

- Self-awareness and Adaptability—resilient; has personal modesty and humility; willing to learn from others; patient, optimistic, flexible, and adaptable

- Results and Performance Driven—assumes personal ownership and accountability for business results and solutions; consistently delivers results that meet or exceed expectations; makes the customer central to all thinking; keeps the focus on driving customer value

v2. 02/08/06

© Johnson & Johnson Services, Inc.

Reprinted with the permission of Johnson & Johnson Strategic Talent Management

- The Websites for the companies competing with the organization that has the position you want. Go to the "Careers" section of their Websites, and look at competencies listed in each of their IT project manager positions.

- Employment advertisements for similar positions in newspapers and association publications to see if they have listed competencies.

- Your professional association Website. (For project management, you would want to go to *www.pmi.org* if you live in the United States, to *www.apm.org.uk* in Great Britain, or to an equivalent site for your own country. For human resources, go to *www.shrm.org*.) Look at job opportunities listed to see if the organization has identified competencies for the position. Also, check out the research capabilities of the association. Information about key professional competencies may be available online or by calling a research professional on the organization's staff.

- The Website of the organization itself. See if you can find information about the corporate culture to help you identify which competencies seem to be valued. One area that can give you insight into the culture is if they have information about the organization mission, vision, or values posted online or available in other organization publications. Read annual reports—particularly focusing on letters from the chairman and CEO. See if you can determine what the organization values or where the organization is having problems (or feeling pain). Learn more about the organization from other sources. Look for clues indicating the competencies the organization needs now and will need in the future to be successful.

> **Key Point**
>
> Notice that the approach used in this book is different from the traditional approaches to getting ready for an interview. The competency-based interview approach, like the competency-based resume approach, always looks at the employer's needs first. Then you are encouraged to think about how you fit what the employer is looking for—the critical competencies the employer needs—to be successful now and in the future.

Analyze online or traditional advertisements and job postings, and focus on words that might be on an organization's list of competencies organization-wide or for a particular position. Remember that most of the competencies can be stated several ways—most words have synonyms.

Take the time to identify the most relevant competencies for the specific position by starting with core, department or functional, and individual competencies that have been identified for your professional area. Most organizations typically identify between eight and 12 of the most critical competencies for most positions to make it easier for managers and employees to track and evaluate the information.

> *One way to help yourself think about this is to simply ask the question, "What competencies would I look for if I was the hiring manager?"*

Also spend a few minutes thinking about the level of expertise in each competency needed to be successful in the position, and what kind of experience you can mention to prove you have that competency *at the right level*. Many of the more sophisticated organizations evaluate your level when they are listening to your answers to interview questions and watching your nonverbal communication.

> According to Signe Spencer from the Hay Group, the 10 most standard competencies being used by organizations are:
>
> 1.   Achievement/Results Orientation
>
> 2.   Initiative
>
> 3.   Impact and Influence
>
> 4.   Customer Service Orientation
>
> 5.   Interpersonal Understanding
>
> 6.   Organizational Awareness
>
> 7.   Analytical Thinking
>
> 8.   Conceptual Thinking
>
> 9.   Information Seeking
>
> 10.   Integrity
>
> These competencies are not listed by rank order. They are simply the 10 most common.
>
> Adapted from *Competency-Based Resumes*, page 28

When an organization's needs change, the competencies needed may also change. Consider how radically different the Federal Emergency Management Agency's (FEMA) needs were one week before, and one week after, Hurricane Katrina hit Louisiana and the Mississippi Gulf Coast in late August 2005. Dealing with a major crisis on a larger scale than we are used to can cause *what it takes to be successful to change*. Most of us watching the response saw that government agencies at the federal, state, and local levels did not respond well. They were not successful in how they handled the crisis.

In other examples, a new CEO may decide to change the strategy of the company—from being the lowest-cost producer to the highest-quality producer. The technical and business competencies needed by the company may need to change to make the new strategy successful.

A consulting firm or a law firm may get a major new client that insists on better customer service than the firm is used to providing. Suddenly, the entire firm must learn the latest customer service information, and evidence of strong customer service may help certain employees have a faster track to partnership.

Even considering these reasons for an organization to review its list of competencies and consider prioritizing them differently, it is still reasonable to expect that the majority of the 10 standard competencies would be listed as competencies for most organizations.

When we look at each competency, though, it is important to remember that different levels of knowledge, skills, and abilities are needed to be successful depending on the level of the position in the organization. For example, we would expect a senior vice president of human resources at a major company to be much stronger in organizational awareness (political savvy) than a recent college graduate just starting to work in human resources.

Organizations typically identify three to five competency levels and can use different terms to describe them. At Penn State University, for example, the levels are baseline, intermediate, proficient, advanced, and mastery.[1] Many senior-level managers in an organization may be rated the equivalent of the advanced level on some competencies, intermediate or proficient in others, and receive the mastery rating in only one area, if at all.

Some organizations choose to recognize the differences expected based on level within the organization by weighting the competencies one way for a junior level professional and another way for managers in the same functional area. The example in the box shows you the way one competency—planning and organizing—can be explained differently for a supervisor, middle manager, and senior manager.

Competency Levels: Planning and Organizing

Competency definition: The ability to visualize a sequence of actions needed to achieve a goal and to estimate the resources required. A preference for acting in a structured, thorough manner.

Individual Contributors to Supervisors

- Manage own time and personal activities.

- Break complex activities into manageable tasks.

- Identify possible obstacles to planned achievement.

Middle Managers

- Produce contingency plans for possible future occurrences.

- Estimate in advance the resources and time scales needed to meet objectives.

- Coordinate team activities to make the best use of individual skills and specialties.

Senior Managers

- Identify longer-term operational implications of business plans.

- Effectively plan utilization of all resources.[2]

Because organizations may identify different competencies, and functions and departments within organizations may have different needs, a more complete list of competencies is included in Appendix A.

Step 4: Select the Most Critical Competencies for the Position

Read through the competencies included in Appendix A very carefully. Mark the competencies that are the most significant for the position you are interested in. Then go back and edit the list to choose the competencies that you think the hiring manager would select. Identify the 10 to 20 most important.

At this point, you've selected the competencies that would be the most critical for the position. Decide if there are some functional/departmental or individual position competencies that you think the hiring manager might put on the list. For example, if you are interested in a sales professional role, is there a possibility that in addition to achieving results, territory management might be critical for success? Do you think the engineering manager hiring a chemical engineer for a plant might be interested in your knowledge of statistical process control?

Because most organizations identify between eight and 12 competencies for each position, my suggestion is to identify 10 to 15 competencies. This will improve the chance that your list includes the competencies the organization selected. Look through the list and think about how important the competency is toward being successful in the position. Because many organizations weight the competencies based upon importance, it is worth spending some time to consider which competencies deserve the most emphasis.

While recognizing that organizations may define different levels of expertise for each competency, I believe that the best way to write a competency-based resume or to prepare for a competency-based interview is to:

- Identify the most critical competencies for the position.

- Think about how to explain your accomplishments to prove that you have a high level of experience in the key competency areas.

So at this point, you've put together a good list of competencies for the particular position you want. Keep trying to improve the list—through research or by asking your networking contacts.

Great work! You've completed the first major part of getting ready for a competency-based interview. Now we are ready to begin working on the next step to help you succeed in a competency-based interview.

Key Points for Chapter 2	
"The competency-based approach always looks at the employer's needs first."	
Key Questions	**Answers**
What are the first steps towards identifying the *right* competencies to help you prepare for a competency-based interview?	Think first about the obvious competencies for the position.
	Then look at the advertisement, posting, or job description from the organization. More organizations than ever before are being direct and listing the competencies they need—especially in their online ads.
What other resources can help employees identify competencies for interviews within their organization?	The organization's Website. Performance appraisals for the position. Employee handbooks and other internal organization manuals. Colleagues working in the relevent department or in the position itself.

Key Questions	Answers
If the organization didn't provide a list of the competencies they are looking for: How do you get started compiling your own list of key competencies? Where do you find some clues as to what these competencies could be?	• Think about what competencie would be obvious for the position. • Look at advertisements and postings from competitors for equivalent positions to see if they have directly listed the competencies they've identified for the positions. Then try to determine if the same competencies work for the position you are interested in. • Visit various employment Websites like Monster.com or CareerBuilder.com and look at equivalent jobs for competency lists. • Look at the Websites for companies that are competitors to the organization tha0t has the position you want. • Read through your professional association Website thoroughly. • Find employment advertisements in newspapers, association publications, and other sources to see if you can glean what are typical competencies for the professional area. • Go to the Website from the organization you are interested in and read through their publications to find information giving you clues about their culture and values.

Key Questions	Answers
What are some of the most typical competencies used by organizations?	Here's a list of the most standard competencies used by organizations: 1. Achievement/Results Orientation 2. Initiative 3. Impact and Influence 4. Customer Service Orientation 5. Interpersonal Understanding 6. Organizational Awareness 7. Analytical Thinking 8. Conceptual Thinking 9. Informational Seeking 10. Integrity Remember these are the most standard and are by no means the only competencies that may be desired by your target organization. Each organization develops its own list of competencies, and the list can be dramatically different based upon the culture and goals of the organization.

Never ascribe to malice that which can be adequately explained by incompetence.

Chapter 3

Know What Interviewers Are Trained to Look For

You got to be careful if you don't know where you're going, because you might not get there.
—Yogi Berra

To add a new interpretation to Yogi Berra's point, when you don't know what to expect in your job search, you are unlikely to do as well in your interview and get the offer. This chapter will give you some ideas about what interviewers in the best companies are trained to look for today.

Knowing what interviewers want can give you a significant edge when you are preparing for an interview as long as you are smart enough to use the information the right way. Always consider the organization's needs first, then how you match those needs. Before the interview, *you* need to think about how you can provide evidence to the interviewer that you are *competent* in the areas the organization needs to be successful.

We'll first cover some of the basics included in interviewer training. What does any interviewer look for with any candidate? What are the types of questions that organizations don't want interviewers to ask—because they might lead to lawsuits or discrimination charges? Then we'll talk about how competency-based interviewing builds on these basics to provide interviewers with more structure and a new and better way to evaluate candidates. The goal is to help the interviewer recognize when the candidate has the key characteristics—or competencies—that it takes to be successful in a particular job or in an organization.

Remember this quote from Aristotle Onassis: "The secret to success is to know something nobody else knows." Once you have succeeded in your interview, you may choose to share some of the secrets of interviewing well with others. I hope you do. Or even buy them a copy of this book. But that is your decision.

What Have Interviewers Always Been Looking For?

The answer is simple: the best candidate for the job. That has not changed. Interviewers are *expected* to identify strong candidates through the interview process, offer them a position, and then encourage the candidates to accept the offer. It may help you, as a candidate, to realize that interviewers only look good when they find someone good enough to get the offer.

> *Good interviewers want you to do well in your interview—their whole job is to get someone hired. They don't look good to their organization when they eliminate all candidates.*

Traditionally, most interviewers look for three things:

1.   Can you do the job?

Do you have the right experience and education to do the work? Many interviewers focus their questions in this area. They don't realize that most employees who eventually leave organizations actually do have the right background, but may not have the discipline, determination, communication skills, or interpersonal skills to be successful.

2. Will you do the job?

You may have a great educational background and the best technical experience, but you may be lazy. Being disciplined, hard-working, and determined still counts for quite a bit with most interviewers.

3. How well do you *fit* with their people, department, organization, and culture?

This is the category that covers your social skills and communication style. You may have the best education and experience. You might be someone who takes work seriously and works very hard. Or you may be an absolute jerk who can't work well with other employees. You may think you are smarter or better than other employees. You may just have poor communication skills that get you in trouble at work. Or you may simply have a different personality than most of the other, more arrogant employees. These things matter to managers because most of them have spent more time than they wanted dealing with conflicts between employees.

Interviewers will usually make decisions about how well you fit the organization unconsciously. This is the category where your nonverbal communication counts. In any interview, you need to recognize that interviewers are going to be trying to determine:

- Do you have good social skills?

- Are you articulate?

- Do you use good grammar?

- Are you dressed appropriately?

- Do they like you?

- Do you have the same sense of humor as the rest of the group?

- Do you seem to know how to handle yourself appropriately?

- How will your personality *fit* with the people you will need to work with?

More information about the importance of nonverbal communication in the interview process is included in Chapter 6.

What Are Interviewers Taught to Avoid Legal Problems?

Almost all of the better, more sophisticated organizations train their managers, supervisors, and college recruiters to avoid asking questions and behaving in ways that can cause a candidate or an employee to file a discrimination charge or a lawsuit. Most countries, states, and provinces have employment laws in place to protect their citizens and residents against discrimination. When federal and state laws conflict, most good human resources managers encourage their organizations to comply with the stricter law.

In the United States, federal laws (and many state laws) protect against discrimination based on race, sex, age, religion, disability, veteran status, color, and ethnicity/national origin. So questions about your marital status, sexual orientation, religious life, illnesses or injuries, where your family is from, or any other protected type of question should not be asked in the interview. For some examples of illegal questions, please review Appendix C.

Interviewers in the United States are trained to focus the interview on what it takes to be successful on the job and away from the candidate's personal life. Good training programs teach interviewers *not to ask questions* about these "protected" areas unless there is a bona fide occupational reason to do so. An example of a legitimate bona fide occupational qualification? Interviewers selecting a new minister or rabbi. In *that* case and only that kind of case, they would be allowed to ask questions about the candidate's religion or religious views.

Interviewers at government contractors and subcontractors are also trained to give a preference to someone who comes from one of the protected classes when candidates are equally qualified.

In Europe and many other parts of the world, interviewers are more likely to ask questions about the personal life of a candidate as a way to get to know him or her. And it still is not that uncommon for candidates in the United States to tell stories about being asked illegal or inappropriate questions.

Why does this still happen? Interviewers may not have been trained on EEO and diversity, or basic interview skills. Or they may simply think that the laws don't matter and they don't have to follow them. Or they may not be very sophisticated.

As a candidate, you may be asked an illegal or inappropriate question. If you are, put the question in context. Don't take it personally, and don't get angry. Then think about any business need that might be the real reason for the question, and see if you can respond to that underlying need in your answer. Always show respect for the interviewer.

I can remember during an on-campus interview being asked by a vice president of human resources at a major utility company in the Midwest whether I thought I'd ever get married. I knew the question was illegal. I first put the question in context: He had just told me his daughter was in a similar MBA program. I thought that he probably cared a lot more whether his daughter ever married than whether I did.

Then I thought about the underlying business need his question represented: Would he put energy, effort, and financial resources into training me and just have me leave a few years later?

Here is the response I gave him:

I don't know if I'll ever get married. I do know how hard I've worked to get a good education and my MBA. I know how important it is to me to have a good career, and I know that will always be important to me.

Although I didn't go to work for his organization, I did get asked back for a second interview.

If you consider the 79,432 discrimination charges filed in 2004[1] in the United States, you can begin to understand why more organizations are moving toward more structured interviews. Giving interviewers a list of questions to choose from that have already been approved by good human resources and legal departments can significantly reduce the chance that rogue interviewers will ask illegal questions that lead to discrimination charges or lawsuits.

Competency-based interviews are highly structured and provide interviewers with a list of three to five primary questions in each competency area. One significant benefit? Competency-based interviews reduce the probability of an interviewer asking a candidate illegal and even inappropriate questions. Most employers would probably say, though, that the main benefit of competency-based interviews is their focus on the competencies the organization or department really needs to be successful.

Joe Gorczyca, Senior Director–Human Resources at HP, is responsible for human resources for the company's worldwide sales and global supply chain organizations. At HP, he says, "In addition to focusing on competencies required for job performance, we try to focus on competencies that reinforce the corporate culture."

If you think about the benefits to an organization, it is easy to understand why competency-based interviews have become the standard.

How Are Interviewers Trained Differently for Competency-Based Interviews?

In addition to spending time talking about interviewing basics and EEO and affirmative action concerns, training to conduct competency-based interviews:

- Focuses on the key competencies for a particular position and core competencies for the organization.

- Helps the interviewer know what to listen for and observe to be able to assess the candidate more accurately.

One of the most important core competencies at Johnson & Johnson is *Integrity and Credo-based Actions*. According to Uneeda Brewer-Frazier, Director of Management Education and Development at the company, "Because of the strong credo-based culture at Johnson & Johnson, we work hard to select people who treat other employees and customers with respect, don't cut corners, and demonstrate integrity through their work and actions. It is so important within Johnson & Johnson that it really impacts every aspect of how we do business and how we treat people."

Johnson & Johnson trains interviewers about their competencies and provides them with an interview guide that includes a list of planned behavioral questions for each competency. Interviewers are encouraged to ask follow-up questions to probe for additional information when an explanation isn't complete or the response is unusual or unclear.

So the interviewer, after going through the introductions and clarifying some things in the candidate's background, begins the main part of the interview with a competency-based question. In addition to the example included in this chapter on *Integrity and Credo-based Actions*, you might want to review the example in Chapter 1 on the competency *Results and Performance Driven*.

The interviewer is asked on the following Johnson & Johnson form to write about the candidate's answers. Specifically, the interviewer is asked to look at the three main parts of any answer to a behavioral question: Situation/Task, Action, and Result (STAR). Because these three parts are looked at carefully by most interviewers from organizations using behavioral interviewing, it is important to understand what the interviewers need to identify.

1. Situation/Task. What is the basic situation, task, or problem that you are giving to answer the behavioral question? Expect to give the details. (Note: Some organizations use the word *Problem* instead of *Situation* or *Task*.)

2. Action. What action did you take to make the situation better? What decisions did you make to handle the task or resolve the problem?

Integrity and Credo-Based Actions	Key Examples
Lives and champions our Credo-values; displays command of one's self and responsibilities; strong personal integrity; creates and maintains an environment of trust.	☐ **Transparency**—Does not hold back on what needs to be said. Shares information in a truthful manner.
	☐ **Trustworthy**—Easily gains the trust of others through appropriate ethical behaviors. Behaves consistently in similar situations.
	☐ **Builts trust**—Treats others with dignity and respect. Models the Credo values and holds others responsible for their actions.

Planned Behavioral Questions

1. Tell me about a time at work when you objectively considered others' ideas, even when they conflicted with yours.

2. We do not always work with people who are ethical or honest. Was there ever a time when you observed another employee or direct report do something that you thought was inappropriate?

3. Often there are people in an organization who deserve more credit than they receive. Tell me about a time when you were involved in a situation such as this. How did you handle the situation?

4. Often it is easy to blur the distinction between confidential information and public knowledge. Can you give me an example of a time when you were faced with this dilemma? What did you do?

5. Describe a time when you were asked to do something at work that you did not think was appropriate. How did you respond?

Situation/Task	Action	Result

Communication

Integrity and Credo-based Actions Rating

Reprinted with permission of Johnson & Johnson Strategic Talent Management

3. Result. What was the result of the action? How did it benefit the organization or your department? What did you learn that will help you be even stronger in the future? Any major "lessons learned" for you or your organization? Did you make money for the organization? Did you save time?

Chapter 4 will go into more detail to help you learn how to respond more effectively to behavioral questions using these three areas. (Johnson & Johnson calls it STAR. Many career counselors know this approach under the acronym PAR, or Problem—Action—Result. Others refer to it as Situation—Action—Result, but I'm not aware of any calling it SAR. When an organization wants to look at the result first, be aware that STAR can easily become RATS.)

In a competency-based interview at Johnson & Johnson, the interviewer is asked to look at the candidate's answers in each competency area and rank them according to the following scale:

So the more you can find out about the position and what it takes to be successful in it before the interview, the more likely you are to be able to give the interviewer strong answers that help prove that you would be *competent* in the position.

The interviewer is also asked to assess the candidate's communication skills as shown in the following:

5   Much more than acceptable (Significantly exceeds criteria for successful job performance)

4   More than acceptable (Exceeds criteria for successful job performance)

3   Acceptable (Meets criteria for successful job performance)

2   Less than acceptable (Generally does not meet criteria for successful job performance)

1   Much less than acceptable (Significantly below criteria for successful job performance)

Communication—Clearly conveying information and ideas through a variety of media to individuals or groups in a manner that engages the audience and helps them understand and retain the message.

+	0	–	
❏	❏	❏	Organizes the communication
❏	❏	❏	Maintains audience attention
❏	❏	❏	Adjusts to the audience
❏	❏	❏	Ensures understanding
❏	❏	❏	Adheres to accepted conventions
❏	❏	❏	Comprehends communication from others

Communication Rating ☐

Key Points for Chapter 3	
"If you know what the interviewer is looking for, you will have an advantage your competitors don't."	
Key Questions	**Answers**
Why is it important to know what the interviewer is going to be looking for before you are interviewed?	It can give you a significant edge over other candidates in the interview. Try to identify the employer's needs first, then start thinking about how you can prove to the employer that you have experience and skills in these critical competency areas.
What do interviewers always look for?	The best candidate for the job.
What three main points cover what interviewers are looking for?	1. Can you do the job? 2. Will you do the job? 3. How well do you fit with their people, department, organization, and culture?

Key Questions	Answers
What are the protected classes under United States employment laws?	• Race • Sex • Age • Religion • Disability • Color • Veteran status • Disability/National Origin
As a candidate, what is the best way to handle an illegal question?	• Put the question in context. • Don't take it personally, and don't get angry. • Identify the business need underlying the question, and respond to that business need in your answer.
Why have more organizations moved to structured, competency-based interviews?	1. To reduce the chance that bad interviewers will ask illegal questions during the interview. 2. To help interviewers focus on selecting candidates based on the competencies the organization needs to be successful. 3. To help organizations reinforce and strengthen their corporate culture.
What is included in competency-based interview training?	• Interviewing basics. • EEO and affirmative action/legal and illegal questions. • Key competencies for the position. • Verbal/nonverbal communication. • Assessing candidates on competencies (including communication skills).
What are the three main parts a good interviewer will listen for in a candidate's answer to a behavioral question?	• Situation/Task/Problem • Action • Result
What are the acronyms used by interviewers to describe the three main parts of a good answer to a behavioral interview question?	• STAR—Situation/Task, Action, Result • PAR—Problem, Action, Result

Chapter 4

Expect Competency-
Based Behavioral
Questions

*Plans are only good intentions unless they
immediately degenerate into hard work.*

—Peter Drucker

To take a small amount of license with Peter Drucker's quote, you need to, as a candidate, *plan to work hard* to succeed in a good competency-based interview. Learning to give your best, high-quality answers to the questions isn't easy. Even if you know you are good verbally, you could be *better* if you anticipate what will happen in the interview, and practice. You need to *actively* prepare.

Actors rehearse their lines and movements for weeks before a play or being filmed in a movie.

Medical students and doctors practice surgical techniques on human cadavers. Before a particularly difficult surgery using a different, new technique, surgeons spend hours strategizing and planning.

The best litigators work with mock juries and even go through mock trials before a major trial to help them anticipate the real jury's concerns and issues. The best coaches and players spend hours training, physically and mentally. They identify the other team's strengths and weaknesses, review films of their games, and then adjust their own plays to improve their chance of winning.

Like the best actors, doctors, lawyers, coaches, and players, the best interviewees plan for their interviews and prepare. If they want to work at the most sophisticated companies and organizations, they know they need to anticipate competency-based behavioral questions. If they already work for a competency-based organization, they should be savvy and recognize the need to prepare for their interviews thinking about the competencies needed for the new position—whether it is a promotion or a transfer.

The best interviewees today expect behavioral interview questions targeting the competencies needed to be successful in the position. They focus on the most important competencies the employer is looking for, and then start thinking about how they can prove they are strong in each of these key competency areas.

What Are Competency-Based Behavioral Questions?

Competency-based behavioral questions are questions asking for examples from your past behavior and experience to help the interviewer assess how strong you are in key competency areas.

Remember that the theory behind behavioral questions is that past behavior is the best predictor of future behavior. If the interviewer wants to predict whether you are going to be successful at something in the future, he needs to find out how successful you've been in the past.

Competencies basically provide the interviewer with a target for behavioral interview questions. As an interviewee, you need to be focused on the same target: competencies. If you work this process the right way, the competencies you've focused on are the same competencies the interviewer is targeting.

What Must Be Included When Responding to Competency-Based Interview Questions?

There are three parts to any good answer to a behavioral question:

1. Situation or Task or Problem

2. Action

3. Result

Good interviewers are trained to listen for the three parts of the answer. At Johnson & Johnson, for example, the interviewers are even asked to take notes and provide the candidate's answers by these three areas on their interview evaluation form. See pages 38 and 39.

The best order to talk about the three parts, though, depends on which part of the answer is the most important to the interviewer. If you are interviewing with someone who is very results-oriented, start with the result. If the most critical piece to the interviewer is an understanding of the process, start with the situation or the action.

Spend some time, then, thinking about whether the result or the process will make your point most effectively to the decision-maker—the interviewer. As with any good sale, you need to think about the customer's wants and needs, and make sure that you talk about what is the most important to the interviewer first.

What Is the Best Way to Prepare for Competency-Based Interview Questions?

Take the time to be strategic. Work through this list:

1. Look at the key competencies you've identified for the position you plan to interview for.

2. Think about your strongest accomplishments that prove your *competence*—in each key competency area. Make sure to include at least a few accomplishments that are *not* already on your resume.

3. Pick examples to talk about that show as high a level of competence as possible, unless you are interested in interviewing for a position that you are overqualified for.

4. Then think about how you can explain the accomplishment to the interviewer, using conversational words—whether in English, Spanish, Mandarin Chinese, Japanese, Russian, or another language.

5. Be reasonably concise but also complete with your answers.

6. Remember to be positive and to make sure your nonverbal communication supports what you are saying. Don't give the interviewer a *mixed* message. Read Chapter 6 for more details about nonverbal communication.

How Does This Work?

Here are a few examples to show you how to begin proving your own competence. I've chosen examples from different professional levels, from entry-level to executive. In most cases, the examples the candidates chose to talk about also show they are strong in more than one competency area. See if any of these examples describe something you've done yourself. Pay attention to the way the candidate gives the answer by picking the key points that are the most important to telling the story. Notice that:

● These examples use conversational language.

● The candidates stay focused, without going off on any kind of tangent.

Let's look first at the competency *Initiative*. Other competencies with specific examples are included in Chapter 5.

Initiative

Chief Financial Officer, Healthcare Company, interview with large hospital system.

Question: *Give me an example of a time that you were able to take the lead in changing financial policy or practice for your organization.*

Situation/Problem: When I became the Chief Investment Officer, the senior managers and board were used to taking very little risk with the investment portfolio. The problem at the time was that by playing it so conservative, the returns were lower than I thought they should be.

Action: I spent six months educating key senior managers and board members about the potential benefit of taking at least 15 percent of the portfolio and using hedge funds and other nontraditional investment strategies. I met with them one-on-one and presented my recommendations at the end of the year board meeting.

Result: With support from the Chief Financial Officer and the CEO, I persuaded the board to change the company's investment policy to allow up to 25 percent of the investment portfolio to be invested in hedge funds and other, more esoteric investments.

What competencies are demonstrated in this answer?
In addition to showing initiative, the candidate clearly showed he performed at a high level in these major competencies:

- Achieves Results
- Organizational Awareness/Political Savvy
- Impact and Influence
- Analytical Skills
- Interpersonal Skills
- Conceptual Skills/Strategic Agility

Administrative Assistant, interview for executive secretary position.

Question: *Have you seen the opportunity to do something in your position that would really help the department you supported run more effectively? Tell me about it.*

Problem: When I started working in the sales department, most of the sales representatives kept their own records, and each of the eight territory managers tracked the information in their own spreadsheets. The managers provided the information to me every week, and I was responsible for consolidating the data on a single spreadsheet. I could see that my manager would have much better, more current information if we standardized the spreadsheet department-wide and linked it directly to information the sales representatives entered into the system.

Action: I talked to my manager about why our department should update the way we collected sales information. I suggested how to set this up and volunteered to help him update the system.

Result: I worked with two of the territory managers to design a system that would work using Excel and Access, and had the new system in place in one month. They now have real-time information on the status of any sales prospect, which helps the managers make better decisions.

Other competencies shown in the candidate's answer include:
- Achievement/Results Orientation
- Influencing Skills
- Information Seeking
- Interpersonal Skills
- Analytical Skills
- Organizing

College Senior, Computer Engineering, interviewing for first job after graduation.

As a college senior majoring in computer engineering, Brian had focused on keeping his 3.67 GPA at the University of Maryland and had very little real work experience when I first met him.

One of the best things about competency-based resumes and interviews for less experienced candidates is that they can choose their examples proving they are strong in key competency areas from work, school, or volunteer activities.

Question: *Tell us about a time you demonstrated initiative in school.*

Action/Result: I worked as a key member of the team that won the best senior project in the Computer Engineering honors program this last year. That next week, the department head, who was teaching the class, asked me to review his article based upon our project, before he submitted it to the best technical journal in the field.

Situation/Task/Problem: In my senior honors class, our professor asked us to work in teams of four to decide on a project using the computer engineering skills we had learned in the program. Our group decided to build a robotic fertilizer spreader, and I took the initiative to take the lead with the computer engineering work on the hydraulic system design.

Other competencies demonstrated by the candidate in the answer include:

- Achieves Results
- Analystical Skills
- Information Gathering
- Interpersonal Skills

Communication Tips for More Successful Answers

After reviewing the different ways these candidates showed their initiative, are you beginning to think of some times you've proven that you can demonstrate initiative? You *can* prepare, practice, and do all the things you need to do to build the competency you need to be successful in your next interview. I have confidence. You've already come up with an example or two showing your initiative!

Before we go to the next chapter, here are a few more tips to make your answers even better:

1. Make sure you respond to the question being asked. Don't assume you understand the question before the interviewer is finished talking. Listen.

2. Be smart with the language you choose. When possible, make sure to include the language used by your professional colleagues. Do some research on specific words and jargon used by the employer, and remember to include the employer's language in your answers. Consider using competency-related language in your answer. Know synonyms for each key competency.

3. Expect follow-up questions to your answers. The interviewer may want some additional information. So do your homework and review the details of any project or assignment you may use as an example to provide evidence that you are competent in a key area. Be able to cite financials, statistics, or headcount information if it is related to your example.

4. Once you have brought up a subject, any follow-up question related to what you have said is fair. So be careful and choose examples you are willing to talk about in detail.

5. Use positive language when answering any question. This tip is repeated on purpose because it is very important. Interviewers do not want to offer a job to someone who they perceive thinks negatively and does not take responsibility for his or her actions. Don't be perceived as a victim. Even when something happens to you (instead of you making something happen), you always have the ability to respond with an answer that shows you learned something from the experience.

6. Prioritize the parts of your answer to say the most important—to the interviewer—first. This is simply the best way to make sure the interviewer pays attention to the most convincing part of your answer—before he possibly loses attention. In Chapter 5, you'll be given some examples that will show you how to prioritize as effectively as possible.

Now you are ready to look at a few additional examples of competency-based behavioral questions and learn some more tips that will help you answer these questions more effectively. In the next chapter, you'll learn how to pick good examples to prove your competence in critical competency areas. It takes more than initiative to be successful! But keep using your initiative to learn what you're going to need to ace the next interview. In other words, just keep reading.

Key Points for Chapter 4	
Competencies provide the interviewer with a target for behavioral interview questions. As an interviewee, you need to focus on the same target: competencies.	
Key Questions	**Answers**
Who prepares for interviews?	The best interviewees. The people who will probably get the offer.
What are competency-based behavioral questions?	Competency-based behavioral questions are questions asking for examples from your past behavior and experience to help interviewers assess how strong you are in key competency areas.
What must be included in any good answer to a competency-based interview question?	• Situation/Problem/Task • Action • Result
What is the best way to prepare for a competency-based interview question?	1. Identify the critical competencies for the position. 2. Think about your strongest accomplishments in each key competency area. 3. Consider how to explain the accomplishment to the interviewer using conversational language. Be concise and complete with your answer. Don't forget to cover situation/task/problem, action, and result. 4. Be positive and make sure your nonverbal communication supports the words you are saying.

Key Questions	Answers
What order should you use to talk about situation/problem/task, action, and result?	It depends on which part of the answer is the most important—or the most critical—to the interviewer. As with any sale, you need to be aware of the customer's wants and needs, and talk about the most important part first. Saying this another way, what is most important to the interviewer should take priority over what is most important to you.
What else should you consider when you are getting ready to answer a competency-based interview question?	• Listen well and respond to the question being asked. • Be smart with the language you use in the interview. Remember to use your professional language with your colleagues, and include terms showing that you are comfortable with the terms used in the organization's culture. Use competency-related language. • Be prepared to answer follow-up questions probing your initial answer for additional details or competency-related information. • Choose examples you are willing to talk about in detail. • Use positive language. • Prioritize the parts of an answer and always make your most critical points first. Emphasize what you believe is the most critical to the employer this way.

Chapter 5

Prove Competencies With Examples

After reading the last chapter, you know to expect competency-based interview questions when you interview with the *best* places to work—the more sophisticated companies, government agencies, and nonprofit organizations. You've started to get the idea about how to give good answers to these tough, more focused interview-style questions.

Now we need to build on the information we've already covered. Remember that most of us needed to learn the alphabet before reading. We went to school to learn before we started working. Most of us dated someone before we married him or her. When we wanted to begin jogging or running, most of us started by running a few minutes and slowly building up the time. (On that last point, I admit to personally knowing an exception. I will always remember one of my favorite human resources managers coming into the office and telling me that he'd just run 3 miles on his very first run. He told me he couldn't understand why he was sore, or later, why I said, "You did *what*?" and started laughing.)

In this chapter, you'll learn some special things to think about to help you avoid potential problems when you craft an answer to questions targeting certain competencies. It is always good to know when you are going to fly over the Bermuda Triangle. Or what the unwritten rules are. How to avoid sitting in the wrong person's chair or parking in *their* parking place *they always* park in.

You'll also learn some more ideas about how you can be even more savvy about choosing your best answers to competency-based behavioral questions. How can you identify stronger examples? How can you learn to prioritize what you say in your answer—so you make sure the interviewer listens to and understands the most important point?

Let's Get Ready

- Review the critical competencies. Make sure you understand what it takes to be successful in your own professional area and in the position you are interested in.

- Identify your best examples to provide evidence that you are strong in each key competency.

- If you are having trouble coming up with good examples, ask for help. Your mentors, colleagues, family, and friends may remember some things you've done that demonstrate how competent you are. Remember to only ask people who you know will have good things to say about you.

Note: Some people just seem to have a difficult time talking about their strengths and, instead, look at it as bragging. Modesty is never a virtue in an interview. To be effective in interviews, you need to get over the feeling that it is not okay to talk about your accomplishments. It *is* okay—it is so important that it is actually essential.

> *Modesty is never a virtue in an interview.*

Let's start by looking at more good examples candidates used to answer competency-based interview questions targeting the competencies *Ethics and Integrity* and *Customer Service*. These competencies are two of the most commonly used competencies today according to the Hay Group's Signe Spencer. Thoughtful and complete answers to specific competency-based questions targeting these two competencies can make a definite difference in how the interviewers perceive you.

Ethics and Integrity

Let's say you are interested in interviewing for a position at Johnson & Johnson or another company or organization that you have heard highly values credibility, ethics, and integrity. So you first need to think of examples that demonstrate you're highly ethical and can prove that you are honest and have integrity.

We are all savvy enough to recognize that what we choose to talk about matters—especially when talking about integrity and honesty. People seem to have different definitions of these words. Even philosophers have struggled with answering the question, "What is honesty?"

To illustrate this point just a little, I've chosen someone I know very well who considers herself quite honest. How many times has she told others how good they look when she sees them—when she doesn't really think they look good? In her opinion, these *white lies* aren't being dishonest, as long as she's achieved her purpose of *making the other person feel better*.

In almost all cases, as a candidate, it is important to know that you need to strike the right balance between showing that you are honest and trustworthy without being perceived as judgmental and self-righteous. Most interviewers will respond well to candidates who are matter-of-fact, are, balanced, and can explain what they have learned that will help them make better decisions in the future. Being self-righteous can be perceived as a definite negative, although this may depend on the personality of the interviewer, the position, and the culture of the organization.

Human Resources Professional, Interview for HR Position, Fortune 500 Chemical Company.

Question: *Describe a time when you were asked to do something at work that you did not think was appropriate. How did you respond?*

Situation: I was working on finalizing a chart showing the employee headcount for the different facilities within the division. It was more difficult than usual because the organization had just gone through a restructuring, and transfer and termination dates changed daily. When I explained the situation, my manager told me to "make up the numbers if you have to."

Action: I asked if he could wait 45 minutes—I thought I'd be able to confirm the real numbers by then. He agreed to wait.

Result: I gave him a chart showing accurate employee headcount information 30 minutes later.

College Senior, Nursing, Interview for Labor and Delivery Nurse at a major Chicago hospital

Question: *Describe a time when you were in a situation where you felt something you were asked to do was wrong, unethical, or inappropriate. How did you respond?*

Situation: When I worked as a student nurse at the University Medical Center, I told one of the nurses on the graveyard shift that we needed to get a doctor to sign the order to continue restraints for an alcohol withdrawal patient. She told me that the order wasn't necessary.

Action: I called my professor to ask for advice because I wasn't comfortable ignoring the hospital's policy. Then I decided to go ahead and call the doctor to get the signature before the other order expired.

Result: I was able to make sure we followed the hospital policy—it just made sense to me.

Experienced Attorney, Interview for Appointment in U.S. Army Judge Advocate General's Corps

Question: *Tell me about a time when you had to do something you didn't necessarily agree with.*

Situation: I worked defending a doctor practicing internal medicine who had been accused of medical malpractice by a patient for her failure to diagnose lupus in the early stages of the disease.

The patient was very sympathetic, but I knew it was my job to represent the doctor.

Action: Despite feeling some sympathy for the plaintiff, I stayed focused on the case and represented my client, the doctor, as well as I could.

Result: The case settled out of court. My client told me she was very happy with my work and thought I had done a good job of representing her.

Customer Service

When we think about this competency, many of us think first about customer service professionals. We don't always realize that almost all of us have customers and clients, whether they are the internal customers within our organization or the external customers who keep our organization in business.

This competency is clearly important for most of us. Customers buy our products, use our services, and basically make our whole organization successful. Our internal customers and clients, including the people we report to and departments we support, can also have a direct effect on our careers.

Auditor, Interview for Fortune 500 Company

Question: *Describe a time when you worked on an audit and had to deal with some resistance from the people in the department or company you were auditing.*

Situation: I was assigned to work on a financial audit of 12 retail sites in Los Angeles for one of the major home improvement retail chains. At one of the locations, when I asked for certain inventory records, the employees told me that they were not available. Other information was also "not available."

Action: I spoke with the store manager and told him about the lack of support I was receiving from the employees. He suggested that I talk to all the employees at the store meeting at the beginning of the next shift. I explained to the employees that my job was to conduct the audit, and I'd appreciate their help. I asked if they had any questions about how the audit process worked, and answered a few of their questions.

Result: I was able to complete the audit and develop a good relationship with managers and supervisors at that particular store.

Director, Fundraising, Interview for Vice President, Fundraising at National Organization's Headquarters

Question: *Tell me about a time you persuaded a donor to contribute to the organization even though their first answer was "no."*

Result: We just found out two weeks ago that one of the largest foundations in the city is donating $500,000 to the nonprofit's capital campaign.

Situation: As a fundraiser, I've learned to never take no as an answer until I've heard it at least three times. So I'm used to having the first response be negative. Last year, we were told no for the second time by the foundation.

Action: I talked to one of the women I know who is heading a major fundraising campaign for the nonprofit and asked for her advice. She's very powerful, runs a major law firm, and knows most of the important people in the city. She told me to call one of the key players on the foundation board and use her name. I went to lunch with the board member three times over the next six months, asked for advice, and made the case for donating to the nonprofit.

Waitress, High School Graduate, Interview for Position as Floor Manager for Restaurant Chain

Question: *Tell me about a time you used your best customer service skills.*

Situation: We were opening the restaurant for lunch one day last December, and the back section of the restaurant was really cold. One of the customers asked to speak to the floor manager to ask why they were seating people in such a cold room. I told the floor manager about the problem, and he went to speak to the customer. I looked at the customer while she was talking with the floor manager, and I could tell she was not happy.

Action: After the floor manager left, I talked with the customer and asked if there was anything I could do. I offered her a hot drink and soup, and I didn't charge her for them.

Result: The customer talked to our regional vice president in Dallas and explained what had happened. Our restaurant manager showed me the letter she wrote talking about what a good job I had done handling a difficult situation.

Focus on Organizations That *Match* Your Own Values

Imagine how helpful it would be to know something about the employer's values first, before you are going to give them an answer to a question about your own ethics. Just as they are going to be assessing whether your sense of integrity or ethics *fits* their culture, you benefit by doing your homework and knowing about how well the organization's values *match* your own values.

Start paying attention to public information about organizations and to what people are saying about them. Every year, big corporations are ranked based on corporate reputation. In Houston, many of us who chose to listen to our personal contacts heard questions about Enron's reputation several years before it became international news for its business practices. Make sure *you* choose to listen.

Giving Good Answers to Competency-Based Interview Questions

You've read through the answers good candidates gave to competency-based questions targeting the competencies *Customer Service*, and *Ethics and Integrity* in this chapter, and on *Initiative* in the last chapter. Are you starting to get a little more comfortable with the process? What do these answers have in common?

- They're good at explaining the situation, action, and result in enough detail that the interviewer can tell what the interviewee is talking about, but not so much detail that the interviewer loses the main points.

- The answers are focused on the most important points the interviewee thinks are the most critical to the interviewer. In some cases, you will have to make an *educated guess* about which points are going to matter the most to the interviewer.

- The parts of each answer are prioritized based on things such as the field the position is in, the interviewer's style, or their questions. Sales and fundraising, for example, are highly results-driven professional areas. Some interviewers are so crisp and to the point that if you want to be successful, you need to respond to their questions by giving them the bottom-line result first.

- Within each answer, the interviewee has emphasized the most important or relevant point by talking about it near the beginning of the answer. Don't wait until the end of your answer to give the interviewer your best point—the interviewer may have stopped listening by then!

- The language is conversational, not stilted. When they are interviewed, many people almost automatically become more formal in the language that they use. This is a huge mistake because it could cause the interviewer to perceive you as not being very approachable. Remember that, in addition to competencies, one area interviewers will be trying to assess is how well you will fit into their organization or department.

- The accomplishments the interviewees chose to talk about are less controversial and help the interviewer perceive them as smart and savvy. They prove the interviewee's competence in the key areas needed to be successful in the organization.

Avoiding Potential Problems

So how can you increase your chance of success in a competency-based interview?

- Whenever possible, choose examples that will increase the chance you will be perceived in a positive way by the interviewer.

- Try to avoid giving examples that could make the interviewer perceive you in a negative way—or as a victim. Take ownership of the things that have happened at work that are your responsibility whenever possible. Be professional and don't blame others—even if they deserve the blame.

- Even when you are asked about failures or mistakes you have made, always tell the interviewer what you have learned from the experience that will make you more successful in the future.

- Think about your accomplishments from different competency perspectives. This is important because it will help you be ready to answer questions about different competencies. Almost every accomplishment can be explained differently—simply by emphasizing different parts of the accomplishment. Identify the different competencies shown in your examples, and consider how you would tell an interviewer about the accomplishment differently depending on which competency you are asked about.

- Remember to talk about what matters to the interviewer first.

- Be fairly direct and answer the interviewer's question. Avoiding the answer *might* work for politicians, but it rarely helps in an interview.

- Take the time to pause after an unexpected question if you need to think about your answer. Ideally, this should only happen once or twice in the interview if you've really done your homework and prepared. Many interviewees get themselves in trouble because they just start talking—even when they haven't figured out their answer. This is something you are more likely to do if you are an extrovert as I am.

- If you prepare for a competency-based interview the right way, you should be able to answer most questions the interviewer asks. Taking the interview seriously—taking the time to prepare—will make a difference.

- Practice. Find someone who is a savvy career coach, manager, or human resources professional who can help you fine-tune your answers to competency-based interview questions. Please check them out thoroughly and *make sure they are really competent*. Many people think they are more sophisticated than they really are as a coach or consultant in this area.

What's Next?

When you're getting ready for your next competency-based interview, make sure you start with a list of the competencies for the position. Then go through the list and identify your best accomplishments, providing evidence that you are strong in each competency area. Think about what you want to emphasize and how to explain the answer in a clear, organized, and conversational way. Recognize that there are different ways to give the answer, depending on which competency you want to emphasize. Make sure you have included the three main parts of any good answer: situation/task/problem, action, and result. You will need to think about which order to talk about them, and which part will make your point the most effectively to the interviewer.

My best advice? Don't wait for your next interview. Start working on your list of good, competency-based accomplishments now.

Key Points for Chapter 5	
Modesty is never a virtue in an interview. *Avoiding the answer might work for politicians,* *but it rarely helps in an interview.*	
Key Questions	**Answers**
How can you prove your competencies?	Give the best examples from your experience that demonstrate the competencies for the job.
How can you find organizations that match your own values of competencies?	Look for news stories and surveys on corporate reputation. Talk to your network of colleagues and friends to learn more about an organization you are interested in. Listen.

Key Questions	Answers
What's the best way to prepare for a competency-based interview?	• Review the critical competencies. Make sure you understand what it takes to be successful in your own professional area and in the position you are interested in. • Identify your best examples to provide evidence that you are strong in each key competency. • If it is difficult to develop good examples, ask your mentors, colleagues, managers, family, and friends for their input on times they have seen you demonstrate particular competencies.
What are the key characteristics of good answers to competency-based interview questions?	Good answers: • Explain the situation, action, and result in enough detail that the interviewer can tell what the interviewee is talking about, but not so much detail that the interviewer loses the main point. • Focus on the most important points that the interviewee thinks are most critical to the interviewer. The interviewee may have to make an *educated guess* about which points matter the most. • Emphasize the most important or relevant point by talking about it near the beginning of the answer. • Use conversational, not formal, stilted languge. • Show you are a smart and savvy employee. Whenever possible, choose less-controversial accomplishments and answers tquestions. Always focus on the key competencies needed to succeed in the organization.

Chapter 6

Look Like a Strong Candidate

*Even the smallest person
can change the course of history.*
—Galadriel, *The Lord of the Rings:
The Fellowship of the Ring*

You've worked hard and thought about good answers to behavioral questions targeting the competencies for the particular position you are interested in. That's the first step to being successful in a competency-based interview.

But it is only the first step. You also need to look the part, act the part, and come across to the interviewer as a strong candidate. In this chapter, I'm going to cover the basics that you need to know about nonverbal communication to do well in any interview. Then I'm going to look at how you can work with nonverbal communication in competency-based interviews.

Good, positive nonverbal communication is always a large part of being successful in *any* interview, including competency-based interviews. What is nonverbal communication? Every type of communication we use to send a message except the actual words we choose.

Nonverbal Communication in Any Interview

Nonverbal communication is very important in the interview. So to be successful in any interview, in addition to your strong, competency-based answers, you need to:

- Maintain good eye contact.

- Dress appropriately.

- Use the right gestures.

- Have a good, firm handshake.

- Behave appropriately.

- Smile at appropriate times.

- Respect your interviewer's personal space.

- Respond to your interviewer's nonverbal communication.

- Avoid giving a mixed message where your nonverbal communication contradicts your words.

- Deliver your answers in an organized way.

- Talk with your interviewer in a conversational way.

Looking the part starts with dressing appropriately. Even though you may want to dress differently based upon the culture of the organization or the location of the interview, you are almost always going to be perceived as dressing appropriately if you dress on the conservative end of the range for your professional area. You want the interviewer to remember you because you're so impressive—not because of what you wore to the interview.

One more comment: Pay attention to your voice and diction. Make sure your interviewer can hear you but that you aren't screaming at her. Speak clearly, put some energy and life in your voice, and use good grammar. Try to minimize the number of pauses and what communication professors call dysfluencies (the *uhs, ums, you knows*, and *likes* that sometimes interfere with conversation).

You may have taken a communication class in high school or college or just simply be smart and already know how important nonverbal communication is in any interaction with another person.

First impressions matter, and the interviewer's first impression is based on nonverbal communication. Most interviewers make up their minds quickly about candidates—within the first 15 seconds to two minutes of the interview, depending on the communications.

Clearly, nonverbal communication can make a significant difference in any interview.

> One of my clients, with 10 years of good experience and a Ph.D. from one of the top U.S. engineering programs for his field, told me he'd never done well in interviews. When I met him, he sat on the edge of his chair, leaned forward, and slightly bounced as he was talking. I videotaped him so he could see for himself what he was doing. I explained to him about how important it was to not invade the interviewer's space and told him to sit back in his chair, with his back straight, and to stop bouncing. He followed the advice and received an offer after the next interview.

Remember the saying "actions speak louder than words." Every culture seems to have an equivalent saying, so know that nonverbal communication is important worldwide. Because nonverbal communication is influenced by culture, the *right* nonverbal communication to use in any interview, will be different in Japan or Nigeria than it is in most situations in the United States.

One example of this? Direct eye contact is expected in the United States and is looked at as a sign of honesty and trustworthiness. In certain countries in Africa and Asia, direct eye contact is a sign of disrespect. If you live or work in one of the more diverse cities in the United States or other countries, you may want to learn to be more aware of nonverbal communication differences across cultures. If you use good nonverbal communication in your interview and try to be more sensitive to the cultural needs of your interviewer, it can only work in your favor.

In this chapter, the examples and explanations are based on nonverbal communication in the United States. If you live in another country or plan to interview with an organization based in another part of the world, please take the time to learn what is expected of a good interviewee there—how the interviewers you will be talking with would *perceive* good nonverbal communication. Many places are further from Kansas than Oz was for Dorothy. Remember that the Munchkins spoke and sang in English, and the wizard was from Omaha.

Competency-Based Interviews and Nonverbal Communication

When you are getting ready for a competency-based interview, one of the most important things to remember is to consider the interviewer's and the employer's needs first. By first identifying the competencies the employer needs to be successful, you can begin to think about your own accomplishments to prove you are strong in each competency area.

But in addition to coming up with good answers to competency-based questions, your nonverbal communication needs to be consistent with what you are saying. You can't expect an interviewer to respond positively to your answer if you are rolling your eyes upward while you are giving a good competency-based answer.

When your nonverbal communication contradicts your verbal message, interviewers believe the nonverbal message. So when you tell the interviewer you are willing to relocate but your head is shaking "no," the interviewer, with good reason, is going to question your verbal answer and believe the headshake. When you give an interviewer this type of mixed message, you may be contributing to the interviewer's perception that she cannot fully trust you to tell her the truth. Good interviewees don't give mixed messages in the interview.

What nonverbal communication really matters in a competency-based interview? To provide you with especially helpful tips, I'm going to include anything that could cause the interviewer's perception to be influenced by something other than the specific accomplishment and the words the interviewee is using in the answer.

Let's look at three of the most common competencies and think about the verbal and nonverbal communication we would expect, competency by competency. By thinking about what interviewers would expect to notice to help them assess a candidate's competencies, you can begin to assess your own verbal and nonverbal communication strengths and weaknesses.

> If you begin to be aware that you may be inconsistent with your verbal and nonverbal responses, you may choose to adjust your verbal answer, change your own attitude, or ask for some help from a friend, coach, or other professional to help you understand what might be behind the mixed message—and eventually help your verbal and nonverbal messages be more consistent.

Achievement/Results Orientation

What would a strong interviewee do or say to help prove to the interviewer that he is results-oriented? In many cases, the interviewers themselves might not recognize the specific details that helped them come to the conclusion about a candidate's strength in this competency.

Think about the evidence an interviewer would look for to help prove an interviewee is focused on performance, goals, objectives, or results. In addition to the quality of the answers, a good interviewer would watch for other evidence to help support his assessment of the candidate on the achievement/results orientation competency.

Some of the key evidence is verbal—the words the candidate uses. And some of the evidence is nonverbal. This includes how the candidate:

- Talks
- Maintains eye contact
- Handles body language
- Dresses
- Grooms and takes care of himself or herself

Does the candidate explain the results using numbers, statistics, dollars, time, or other parameters to help the interviewer understand the size or scope of the accomplishment? Someone strong in this competency would. An astute interviewer would expect the answers from a results-oriented candidate to be organized, logical, concise, and complete. The emphasis in some of their most important answers would be on the results instead of the process. The interviewer would be able to tell that it was a priority for the candidate because:

- The result would be given near the beginning of the answer.

- More time would be spent explaining the result than the situation/task/problem or action.

What else helps confirm the candidate is strong in the *Achievement/Results Orientation* competency? A good interviewer would expect a results-oriented person to get to the point quickly. He would generally not be guilty of *wasting the interviewer's time* by going off on tangents not critical to the answer. He would maintain good eye contact. He would be engaged in the conversation. The interviewer would be able to assess this through his gestures, his facial expressions, and the way he sat straight in the chair or leaned very slightly forward. (*Never* lean forward more than just slightly, because you may be perceived as invading the interviewer's space or as simply strange.)

When you think of the people you know who achieve results, what other verbal and nonverbal clues would *you* expect?

Impact and Influence

An interviewer would expect to see many of the same verbal and nonverbal cues discussed for a results-oriented candidate in a candidate strong in impact and influence. As the interviewee who just demonstrated his or her ability to achieve results did, an interviewee demonstrating her influencing strengths would maintain good eye contact, be engaged in the conversation, and sit and stand appropriately.

What are the differences? Remember that this is the competency looking at a candidate's ability to persuade, convince, impact, and influence the people he or she needs to be successful. The differences can be subtle. Think about people who are called aggressive and those who are assertive. Assertive people are equally people-focused and task-focused; aggressive people focus on achieving the goal. Think about the difference in competencies needed to sell to clients based on building strong long-term relationships and simply based on immediate contact and volume. People with strong influencing skills are almost always assertive—not aggressive. They recognize they will need to work with the same people in the future, and they try to protect the relationship if they can.

What evidence would an interviewer notice to help confirm that the candidate had strong influencing skills? Listen to the way the candidate answers the questions and targets the interviewer's real needs. He or she may even ask the interviewer a question to clarify those needs or wants. He emphasizes what they offer that the interviewer is looking for—how his experience will help ensure his success in the new position. In other words, he knows how to sell himself and his ideas, without overselling.

People with strong influencing skills know how to read people and convince them to change their position now or eventually. Their verbal and nonverbal skills can help them be subtle enough to set things up so that the other person even thinks the change is his or her own idea. They can use a short tangent or tell a story, just to help them persuade someone to change their view.

There's also a strong possibility the candidate with strong influencing skills has a good sense of humor. Knowing how to come up with a good one-liner or tell a joke at the right time can help someone relieve tension, persuade a colleague, or close a deal. *Be appropriate: You need to make sure you are not the only one who finds something funny.*

Integrity and Ethics

What verbal and nonverbal clues do candidates give during an interview to help the interviewer assess how strong they are on the competency *integrity*? Astute interviewers may notice that the candidates they assess as lying:

- Give examples that don't make sense or contradict each other.

- Use nonverbal communication that contradicts their words.

- Fidget and avoid eye contact at certain relevant times.

- Move less than candidates telling the truth.

- Talk more slowly and make more speech errors than most candidates.

- Use fewer words when answering questions, often one-word answers with little elaboration.

- Pause longer before answering questions and use longer pauses throughout their communication.

- Use more "generalizing terms" such as *you know what I mean* and *you know* at the end of their sentences.

- Use fewer concrete terms and refer less frequently to specific people and places.

- May guard their mouth, touch their nose, and rub their eyes.[1]

These are just some of the nonverbal ways that good communicators identify lying or deceit. Most good interviewer training will encourage interviewers to look for several indicators to support that someone is not telling the truth. Any single behavior or nonverbal indicator is generally not enough to decide someone is lying. Even law enforcement officers need more than fidgeting and pausing to build their case when they can tell a suspect is not telling the truth. They look for more evidence.

But it is important, as a candidate, to realize that in the interview, you'll generally do better if you tell the truth—because smart and savvy interviewers will probably be able to tell when you choose to lie. As a coach, though, I'm a believer in *diplomatic honesty,* not *brutal honesty.* Tell the truth but say it in a way that is more likely to help you than hurt you. Put the best possible *spin* on what you are saying. Here's an example. For certain people reading this chapter, please know that you don't have to come out and tell the woman in your life that what she's wearing makes her look fat when she asks you. Just ask her what she thinks or tell her that she always looks good to you.

When you think about all the verbal and nonverbal clues that can cause you to be perceived as lying, you'll begin to realize why I have encouraged you to give specific concrete answers to competency-based questions, and to prepare, so you can think about what to say before the actual interview. By taking the time to get ready for a competency-based interview, you'll increase the chance that you won't have to pause or inadvertently give the interviewer another nonverbal indicator that you may not be telling the truth.

Trust me. I *am* telling you the truth.

Other Competencies

After learning more about how to support your answers to competency-based interview questions with good nonverbal communication for the competencies *Achievement/Results Orientation, Impact and Influence,* and *Integrity and Ethics,* you need to think about how to support the other relevant competencies through your nonverbal and verbal communication.

For example, consider the competency *Customer Service.* Wouldn't you expect to see a good customer service or sales professional know when to:

●   Smile and demonstrate support for a customer?

- Pace his or her answers more slowly and use a calmer tone of voice when dealing with a difficult customer?

Think about what evidence you need to provide to be consistent with your verbal answers to competency-based interview questions targeting the other key competencies on your list for the particular position you want or the organization you want to work for.

Other Nonverbal Tips

We may be too old to grow except in pounds, worth, and wisdom. Some things that affect how we look can't be changed. But other things can. If you are a woman who wants to interview for a powerful job, consider getting your makeup done, a new suit, new shoes, and your hair done by someone who knows what he or she is doing. If you need to lose some weight, start your diet and exercise program soon enough to make a difference before the interview. Get recommendations for makeup artists, manicurists, hair stylists, personal shoppers, and good places to shop from other people you know who look polished and professional. It just may be worth the investment.

If you are a man, please consider making some of the same extra effort too. Good grooming is important for both men and women.

Key Points for Chapter 6	
It's not what you say but what you do that matters.	
Key Questions	**Answers**
What is nonverbal communication?	Every type of communication except the actual words someone uses.
What nonverbal communication is important in any interview?	<ul><li>Maintain good eye contact</li><li>Dress appropriately and conservatively</li></ul>

Key Questions	Answers
What nonverbal communication is important in any interview? *(continued)*	<ul><li>Use the right gestures</li><li>Have a good, firm handshake</li><li>Behave appropriately</li><li>Smile at appropriate times</li><li>Respect personal space</li><li>Respond to the interviewer's nonverbal communication</li><li>Avoid giving mixed messages</li></ul>
How does culture affect non-verbal communication?	The *right* nonverbal communication to use will be different based on the country/culture the organization is in, and perhaps the culture of the interviewer. Expect different nonverbal communication when interviewing across cultures, and be more sensitive to the cultural needs of your interviewer. Take the time to learn what is expected of good interviewees by your interviewer—no matter what the culture is.
In addition to the example used to answer a competency-based interview question, what would an interviewer notice that would cause him or her to rate someone as strong in the competency *Achieve Results*?	<ul><li>Does the candidate explain the results using quantitative and qualitative details?</li><li>Are the answers organized, logical, concise, and complete?</li><li>Is the emphasis more on results than process? Do the results seem to be a priority for the candidate?</li><li>Did the candidate get to the point quickly?</li><li>Did the interviewee maintain good eye contact and show that he was engaged in the conversation?</li></ul>

Key Questions	Answers
What would an interviewer expect to notice to help confirm a candidate was strong in the competency *Impact and Influence*?	Many of the same cues shown in the *Achieves Results* competency. The difference? People with strong influencing skills are: ● Almost always assertive, not aggressive, and consider the long-term relationship. ● Able to know how to sell their ideas effectively without selling too much. ● Good at reading people. ● Good at understanding subtleties and using them to convince others. ● Able to use stories and humor to make points and persuade others to change their point of view.
What verbal and nonverbal cues help an interviewer assess a candidate's strengh on the competency *Integrity and Ethics*?	Good interviewers may perceive someone as not telling the truth if they: ● Give contradictory examples. ● Contradict their words with nonverbal communication. ● Fidget or avoid eye contact at specific, relevant times. ● Sit very still and move less than other candidates. ● Talk more slowly and make mistakes verbally. ● Pauses before and during communication. ● Use general terms that imply some knowledge. ● Are less specific, more general, and vague.

Key Questions	Answers
How honest should you be in an interview?	There's no reason to be *brutally honest*. Be *diplomatically honest* instead. Try to explain things using words that will help put the best possible spin on something without being dishonest.
What else should you do to prepare?	• Go through your list of critical competencies for the position and identify what you think the interviewer is going to notice—both verbally and nonverbally—to help justify giving you a strong rating in each competency area. • Make an effort to look as professional as possible the day of the interview. Consider losing weight or buying a new suit or shirt or tie. Get your hair cut if it needs it. Make sure your shoes are shined. Get your makeup done if that is appropriate for the position. If you need some advice, ask the most polished professional person you know.

Chapter 7

Consider Other Important Interview Tips

He who asks a question is a fool
for five minutes; he who does not ask
a question remains a fool forever.
—Chinese proverb

At this point, you've learned about how competency-based interviewing works, how to develop good answers to competency-based interview questions, and how to look and act like the *best* candidate. You probably think you are ready to do well on your next competency-based interview, and so do I—with the addition of the word *almost*.

Because we don't want to be fools forever, we'll follow the advice in the Chinese proverb quoted here and start by asking a question: What else do you need to know to get the offer?

Despite competency-based interviewing being one of the most common approaches to interviewing in today's organizations, you may still find a few questions included in a mostly competency-based interview that are not really competency-based interview questions. Your job as the candidate is to do a good job of answering these questions, in addition to the other questions the interviewer asks you.

Here are five questions you *may* be asked:

● Why are you interested in this position?

● Tell me about yourself.

● What is your current salary? What salary do you expect?

● What are your strengths?

● What is your biggest weakness?

How should you answer these questions to do well in the interview? How can you use your knowledge of competency-based interviewing to give stronger answers to these and other *unexpected* questions?

After reading about how to answer these questions, you'll really think you're ready to be very good on your next interview. Please, though, take the time to review the question-and-answer section at the end of this chapter. You may find that you get just one additional tip that makes all the difference in your next interview. I hope so.

Answer Other Common Questions Showing Competency Strengths[1]

Why Are You Interested in This Position?

You are *very* likely to be asked this question (or a similar question with the same intent) before the interview is set up or during the actual interview itself. Even though this question does not immediately seem that it would belong in a competency-based interview, please know that many interviewers may ask one or two questions that are not in their approved competency-based interview guide.

The best answers to this kind of question focus on how your experience and interests *match* the organization's needs. In other words, this is an opportunity to show you have the *right* competencies for the position and are interested in continuing to develop the competencies that are needed for the organization to be successful in the future.

Here's an example of how to answer the question, "Why are you interested in this opportunity?" "Three main reasons: It will give me the chance to prove how good I am at achieving goals, building strong long-term relationships with customers, and motivating the employees in the department to be even more successful."

Paraphrase the competencies. Explain the relevant competencies using synonyms—in your own words. Expect to give examples of when you've used these competencies in the past. Even when the question is not technically a behavioral question, using past behavior or examples will help provide proof to the interviewer that you will be strong in these same competencies in the future.

Tell Me About Yourself

You have probably recognized by this point that one of the key points made in this book is the need to emphasize the employer's needs first and your own *fit* second. So what is a good answer to "Tell me about yourself"? Think about this: What about you does the employer need to know to realize you have the competencies she needs to help her organization be more successful?

Limit your answer to no more than two minutes. Focus on your work experience. Human resources managers tell unbelievable stories about candidates trying to convert them to another religion during the interview or sharing that they are currently:

- Going through their third divorce.

- Having problems with their children.

- Being treated for cancer and have been told they have six months to live.

You are a professional, and your answer to this question needs to stay professional and away from emphasizing your private, personal life. Please know that this is especially true in the United States. But interviewing, even competency-based interviewing, is affected by the culture of the employer and the laws of the country it is located in. In some other parts of the world, expect questions about your personal life and answer the questions—if you want to do well on the interview. It may be expected.

The traditional answer to this question is chronological: Start from the beginning and work toward the present, emphasizing your background that is the most relevant for the position you are interviewing for. The second approach is to briefly discuss your early background and education, but spend most of the two minutes focused on your current strengths, skills, and abilities, and what you want to do next.

Both approaches can work well for people, but one may be more effective for you, depending on your own situation. Be logical, organized, and concise. Think about mentioning evidence of your competencies that are related to the position you are interviewing for when you are talking about your background—it can help the interviewer begin to understand that you've been developing your competencies over time, and that they are strong.

Remember that the interviewer is probably evaluating your skills as a communicator while listening to the content of your answer.

What Is Your Current Salary?
What Salary Do You Expect?

Many people are extremely uncomfortable answering questions about money in the interview. Talking about money ranks right up there with religion, politics, and sex for many people—as topics they'd like to avoid.

Please remember that one of the main points of competency-based thinking is to focus on the employer's needs first. This is not just about you and what you think is appropriate for the interviewer to ask. When interviewers ask you these types of questions, please realize that they are doing it because, almost always, they need to know. If they want to make you an offer, they need to come up with a salary that you will be happy with and that fits within the range of salaries of people in their organization with similar experience and skills. They are simply trying to be fair.

If you *still* have a problem with answering these questions, please work on getting over it. You need to expect to get at least one question on salary before or during the interview.

So, what's a good answer to these questions? I coach my clients, in most cases, to answer the first question. For the second, I encourage them to tell the interviewer, "I'm sure if you decide that I am the right person for the job that you will do the very best for me that you can do." Guilt is a wonderful thing if it works in your favor.

Please be aware that this is the first step in salary negotiation. To give really on-target advice, a consultant would need to know much more about the job opportunity and your own situation.

What Are Your Strengths?

When you are answering this question, focus first on your strengths that *match* the competencies that are the most important to help the employer be successful in the future. Leave out your strengths that are not important to be successful in the position. For example, if you are very creative and have had your paintings shown in galleries, that type of competency might not be perceived as an asset if you are interviewing for a position as a software engineer.

Choose three or four of the important competencies for the position that you are personally strong in, and answer the question with these competencies. Start with the competency on your list that is the most important for the interviewer's success, and then talk about the competency strength in the second most important area.

Paraphrase and use synonyms to describe the competencies. Take the time to put the competencies into your own language because you will come across as more sophisticated than the next candidate who may just repeat the exact words from the competency list. Actually, you *will* be more sophisticated about how to make competencies work for you than the next candidate. *You* are reading this book!

What Is Your Biggest Weakness?

Listen carefully to the question. Is the interviewer asking for one weakness—or several?

Most career consultants will tell candidates that when they are answering this question, they should pick a weakness and turn it into a strength. That may be true most of the time, but to do this right, you need to remember a few things, to increase your chance of being perceived as having a good answer to this question. You want your answer to be *diplomatically honest*, be original, and be perceived as real to the interviewer. Stay away from the *cookie-cutter* answers such as being a perfectionist, unless you are able to give enough evidence to make it real. Remember that everyone has weaknesses. Saying you do not have any weaknesses simply is not believable.

When you are answering this question, it is important to choose a weakness that is *not* related to the critical competencies for the position. You do not want to be perceived as weak in *analytical skills* if that is a key part of being successful in an accounting position.

Try to pick something that the interviewer may have already noticed as a weakness in the interview. Here's one example to think about: "I'm not always as concise as I think I should be. I'm aware that I need to be better about getting to the point faster, and I'm working on it. I know it is something I could improve." Think about how effective this answer would be for a candidate who has just gone off on a tangent during the interview. At least the interviewer is now aware the candidate recognizes the problem.

Another approach is to focus on something different that might be a little humorous. One client from West Virginia was preparing for an interview in Texas, and he had a good sense of humor. His answer? "I don't know if you've noticed, but some people here think I have an accent. So they underestimate me. While they're doing this, they tell me all sorts of information before they figure out I really know what I'm doing. But occasionally it can work against me." Do you see why this answer worked well for him?

Competency Gaps

In addition to the weakness question, sometimes you may get a question about a competency that you know is not a strength for you—where you have a weakness or a *competency gap*. What can you do, as a candidate, when you recognize that you cannot prove certain key competencies? Or when you are not as strong as you need to be in critical competency areas? As a candidate, you always need to be aware of places that you might have some competency gaps, and start coming up with some ideas about what you can do to overcome the gaps.

One way to handle this type of question is to talk about how you have compensated for the competency gap by using your strength in another competency. For example, it might be hard for you to come up with a time you've directly influenced or persuaded someone to change his or her position on an important issue—but you may be able to *substitute* an example of when you used strong customer service skills.

Another approach to answering the question is to acknowledge the competency gap but to explain what you have done or plan to do to build your strength in the competency in the future. Have you signed up for a class or volunteered for a project at work that will give you the opportunity to prove that you are *competent* in the relevant area in the near future? Let the interviewer know.

Interview Questionnaire: True or False?

1.   The best-qualified candidate always gets the job.

> **False.** Interviewers consider other things in addition to qualifications. They try to assess how willing you are to work hard and how well you'll *fit* into their department and organization. In competency-based organizations, the interviewer will assess how strong you are in the competencies needed to be successful on the job. In addition, interviewers may be persuaded to give an offer to someone who can benefit them politically—say, the nephew of the CEO.

2.   It's a good idea to schedule your first interviews for the positions you are the most interested in.

> **False.** Most interviewees don't do as well in their first interviews as they will in later interviews when they are more comfortable with the interview process. So try to have a "practice" interview (or work with a coach or career consultant) before you have one that really matters to you.

3.   The first few minutes of the interview are the most important.

> **True.** Most interviewers make up their minds quickly.

4.   Wear conservative clothes to an interview.

> **True.** But make sure what you wear is considered conservative for your professional area—not someone else's. It is important to wear conservative clothes because you want the interviewer to remember you for how professional and smart you are and the good quality answers you gave in the interview—not the clothes you wore. If the interviewer remembers you for your clothes, it is *not* a good thing.

5. **Take a planner and a notepad to the interview.**

    Trick question. Take them to the interview but don't pull the notepad out to take notes during the interview. If you take notes during the interview, the interviewer is likely to perceive you as having a poor memory, not paying attention (less eye contact), and perhaps more interested in getting him in trouble (think of a potential discrimination charge or lawsuit). Immediately after the interview, take some notes on your notepad or in your planner—so you can write more effective thank-you notes.

6. **It's always good to arrive 20 to 30 minutes early for the interview.**

    False. In most cases, plan to arrive about five minutes early. If you arrive earlier, realize that you may be inconveniencing the interviewer, who will not expect you to arrive 30 minutes early. Although it *is* better to be early than late, too early is also not good. Get to the location early, but wait in your car, downstairs, or across the street in a Starbucks until the right time to go to the interview. Review your resume and check to make sure you are *still* looking as professional as you were when you first dressed for the interview.

7. **When asked to talk about your background, you should plan to keep your response to about two minutes.**

    True. Don't be too brief—or too wordy. Watch the interviewer's nonverbal communication. If the interviewer is giving you nonverbal cues that she is bored, pick up the pace of your answer and finish talking. Emphasize the competencies that are critical for the position.

8. **During an interview, avoid too much eye contact to help the interviewer be less nervous.**

   False. Maintaining good eye contact is perceived positively in interviews in the United States. Just don't stare!

9. **It is best to be honest and tell the interviewer exactly how you felt about previous supervisors if you are asked for your opinion.**

   False. Remember that diplomatic honesty is better than brutal honesty. If you talk negatively about a former supervisor, the interviewer will think that you will be talking negatively about him in the future. So be professional and discreet.

10. **Don't answer questions about race, sex, age, national origin, marital status, or number of children.**

    Trick question with the true answer, "It depends." Put the question in context and respond considering the underlying reason for the question.

11. **What you mean in your answers to the interviewer's questions counts for more than the interviewer's perception.**

    False. The interviewer will make her decision based on her perception of how successful you will be in the job compared to other candidates. So it is up to you to communicate what you mean as clearly as you can so you can increase the chance the interviewer will perceive you accurately.

12. **Exaggerate your accomplishments, because the interviewer won't be able to tell whether you are telling the exact truth.**

    False. A good interviewer will be able to tell when you are not telling the truth from your nonverbal and verbal communication. Make your best case but make sure you stay honest.

13. **Your job in the interview is to sell yourself.**

    True! Your whole job in the interview is to persuade the interviewer that you deserve a second interview or a job offer.

14. **Preparing for the interview is a waste of time.**

    False. Preparing for the interview is the best use of your time—if you care about being seriously considered for the opportunity.

Key Points for Chapter 7	
When you think you're ready, do a little more.	
Key Questions	**Answers**
Will all the questions in a competency-based interview be competency-based behavioral questions?	Not necessarily. Even during a competency-based interview, you *may* get a few questions that are not traditional competency-based interview questions.
What should you keep in mind when you answer the question "Why are you interested in this position?"	Focus on how your experience and interests *match* the competencies the employer is looking for. A strong candidate would give specific examples to support what he or she is saying.
When the interviewer asks you to "tell me about yourself," what should you do or say?	• Key point: What about you does the employer need to know to realize you have the *right* competencies to help the organization be successful? • Limit your answer to two minutes. Be logical, organized, and concise. • Focus on your professional experience that is relevant to *this* position, not your personal life. • Be logical and follow either the traditional chronological approach or briefly discuss your background and education, and spend most of the time focused on your current strengths and competencies, and what you want to do next.

Key Questions	Answers
How should you answer questions about salary?	• Answer the question about your current salary unless there's a good reason not to. It doesn't matter if it bothers you to tal about money. • Answer the question about your salary expectations by saying something along the lines of, "I'm sure if you decide I'm the right person for the job that you will do the very best you can for me."
What are the most important things to remember when asked to identify your strengths?	• Emphasize your strengths that match the competencies the employer needs to be successful in the future. • Choose three or four of the relevant competencies for the position that are *strengths* of yours. • Start your answer with the competency that has the greatest weight or is the most important to the employer. • Paraphrase and use synonyms to describe the competencies to the employer. Take the time to put the relevant competencies in your own language. • Listen carefully to this and other questions to know whether you are being asked about one strength or strengths with the "s" on the end, which is plural and means you have to give at least two examples.

Key Questions	Answers
What should you consider when asked to identify your biggest weakness?	• Most career consultants tell their clients to pick a weakness and turn it into a strength. To do this right, your answer should be: (1) Diplomatically honest but not brutally honest; and (2) Original. • Choose a weakness *not* related to the key competencies for the position you are interviewing for. • Remember that even the best employees have weaknesses, and you *need* to answer this question. It is not believable to answer this question by saying that you have no weaknesses. • Select a weakness that the interviewer *may* have already noticed in the interview. • Consider picking an example to use that shows some humor and that you are human. Just make sure that you are *not* the only one who thinks it is funny.
What is a competency gap?	A competency you can't prove or a competency you don't have.
How can you answer questions about competencies that fall into the competency gap area for you?	• Talk about how you have compensated by using your strengths in another competency. • Acknowledge the gap and explain what steps you have taken to overcome it. Have you signed up for a class or project, or asked to participate in a project at work that will give you the evidence to *close the gap* for the future?

Key Questions	Answers
What are some other basic tips that you need to know to do well in the interview process?	• Your job in the interview is to sell yourself. • Preparing for the interview is extremely important—if you want an offer. • Recognize that the best candidate doesn't always get the offer. • It is a good idea to schedule interviews for the positions you are most interested in *after* you have had some interviews and know that you are handling the interview well. • Do wear clothes that are considered conservative for your area. • Don't consider taking notes during the interview. Take your notes *immediately after* the interview so you can write more effective thank-you notes. • Plan to arrive 5 to 10 minutes early. • When asked to tell the interviewer about yourself or your background, plan to talk about 2 minutes. • Maintain good eye contact during the interview. • Be professional and discreet when talking about previous employers. • Put any illegal or inapprioriate questions in context and respond considering the underlying reason for asking the question. • Tell the truth but be diplomatically honest and make your best case in your answer.

Chapter 8

Check to Make Sure You Are Ready for the Interview

Step 1: Understand Competency-Based Interview Approaches

Key Questions and Tasks	Reference Page	Complete
Know how a competency-based interview is different from other interviews.		
Review the information about competency-based behavioral interviewing. Begin thinking about how your own behavior has contributed to your success in the past.		

Remember that behavioral interviewing is based on the theory that past behavior is the best predictor of future behavior.

Step 2: Identify the Right Competency List

Key Questions and Tasks	Reference Page	Complete
Review the job advertisement looking for competencies. They may be listed directly as competencies or as success factors, dimensions, or values. Ask for a job description from a recruiter, and see whether the organization has identified competencies as part of that description.		

Key Questions and Tasks	Reference Page	Complete
If the competencies aren't clearly identified in the advertisement or job description, follow these four major steps to develop a list on your own: 1. Think about the obvious competencies for the position. 2. Look at competitors' advertisements and job postings. 3. Check for competencies from other sources, such as employment Websites, newspaper ads, magazines and journals, professional organizations, and the organization's Website. 4. Select 10 to 15 competencies that would be most critical from Appendix A.		

As you research competencies, remember that the competency-based interview approach always looks at the employer's needs first. Your task is to think about how your competencies fit what the employer is looking for.

The 10 most standard competencies used by organizations are: 1. Achievement/Results Orientation 2. Initiative 3. Impact and Influence 4. Customer Service Orientation 5. Interpersonal Understanding 6. Organizational Awareness 7. Analytical Thinking 8. Conceptual Thinking 9. Information Seeking 10. Integrity		
Although this list may be a starting point for you, keep in mind that competencies for a specific organization can be very different based on its culture and goals. Remember, too, that competencies can change as an organization's situation or culture changes.		

Step 3: Understand the Needs of the Employer and the Interviewer

Key Questions and Tasks	Reference Page	Complete
Remember that all interviewers are looking for the best candidate for the job. As a candidate, you can help the interviewer by providing information to demonstrate that you are a strong applicant.		
Begin thinking about how you can prove yourself to the interviewer who is always considering these questions: • Can you do the job? • Will you do the job? • How well will you fit with the organization's culture and people?		
For each competency you have identified as important for the position, be ready to talk about three main elements in your examples. • Situation/Task/Problem • Action • Result Begin to prepare for your interview by outlining these elements for each competency you want to demonstrate.		
Although interviewers are trained to avoid asking illegal questions, this still happens sometimes. **Be prepared to respond to an illegal question.** (An "illegal question" is a question about your status in a "class" that is protected by law, such as race, sex, age, religion, disability, veteran status, color, and ethnicity/national origin.) Try to understand the interviewer's real motivation for asking the question, and respond to the business need that it reflects. Don't take it personally, and don't get angry.		

Key Questions and Tasks	Reference Page	Complete
As you develop your answers to expected interview question, it may be helpful to remember that more organizations are moving toward using competency-based interviews for three main reasons: 1. Competency-based interviews reduce the chances that an interviewer will ask an illegal question. 2. Competency-based questions help the interviewer select candidates with the competencies that the organization needs to be successful. 3. Competency-based interviews help organizations reinforce and strengthen their corporate or organization cultures.		

Step 4: Prepare to Answer Competency-Based Interview Questions

Key Questions and Tasks	Reference Page	Complete
Competencies provide the interviewer with a target for behavioral questions. To be a successful candidate, you need to focus on the same target: competencies.		
Begin to refine your answers to expected interview questions. Responses to competency-based behavioral questions require examples from your past behavior and experience that will help the interviewer assess how strong you are in the key competency areas needed to be more successful in the job.		

Key Questions and Tasks	Reference Page	Complete
To prepare for a competency-based interview: • Identify the key competencies for the position. • Think about your strongest accomplishment in each competency area. • Structure your accomplishments using the situation/task/problem, action, and result framework. • Be concise and complete, and use conventional language in your examples. Use professional terms/language, along with language that reflects the organization's culture, when appropriate.		
Think about your examples from the interviewer's perspective, and be able to restructure your responses. For example, if your interviewer is focused on results, try to start your answers with the "results," followed by information on the situation and your actions. Focus on presenting the most critical information first—*from the employer's perspective.*		
Review these other points when you are preparing your competency-based interview responses: • Listen well, and be sure to respond to the question being asked. • Consider carefully the language you use, so that you present a professional response, but in a conversational, rather than formal, style. Use positive language. • Be prepared to answer follow-up questions to provide additional details or competency-related information. • Choose examples you are willing to talk about, and be prepared to provide detail beyond your planned answer.		

Step 5: Prove Your Competencies With Examples

Key Questions and Tasks	Reference Page	Complete
Your interview responses should always reflect two key points: • *Modesty is never a virtue in an interview.* • *Avoiding the answer might work for politicians, but it rarely helps in an interview.*		
Refine your situation/action/results to make sure you are using the best examples from your personal experience to demonstrate your strength in the relevent competencies for the job.		
Hint: If you have difficulty finding strong examples, ask mentors, colleagues, managers, family, and friends for instances in which you demonstrated particular competencies.		
In competency-based interviews, good responses: • Explain the situation, action, and result in enough detail that the interviewer can tell what the interviewee is talking about, but not so much detail that the interviewer loses the main point. • Focus on points that are, in the interviewee's judgment, most critical to the interviewer. • Emphasize the most important or relevant point by talking about it near the beginning of the answer. • Use conversational, rather than formal, stilted language, and include professional terminology as appropriate. • Avoid controversial accomplishments, and always focus on the competencies that are needed to succeed in the organization and the position.		

Key Questions and Tasks	Reference Page	Complete
Additional suggestions for preparing strong competency-based responses are to: • Be direct, and respond to the interviewer's questions. • Talk about what matters most to the interviewer first. • Choose examples that will help the interviewer perceive you in a positive light. Avoid examples that make you seem to be a victim or "negative thinker." Take ownership of everything that was your responsibility, and don't try to place blame on others, even if they deserve it. • Respond to questions about failures or mistakes by explaining what you learned from the experience that will make you more successful in the future. • Think about your accomplishments from the perspective of different competencies. Almost every situation illustrates more than one competency, depending on which part of the work is emphasized. • If you prepare for the interview correctly, you should be able to answer most of the interviewer's questions. If you need to think about an unexpected question (which should happen only once or twice in an interview), take time to pause so that you can provide a thoughful response. • Practice your answers. Find someone who is a savvy career coach, manager, or human resources professional to help you fine-tune your answers to the most likely questions. Make sure the person you choose understands competency-based interviewing.		

Step 6: Use Good Nonverbal Communication and Look Like a Strong Candidate

Key Questions and Tasks	Reference Page	Complete
Actions speak louder than words. To be perceived as a strong candidate, you need to look and act the part. Focus not just on what you say, but also on how you say it—just as your interviewer will do.		
Think about the competencies required for your target position and the nonverbal communication the interviewer might be looking for with each competency. Remember: Nonverbal communication is *every* kind of communication except the actual words you use. For example, when talking about the competency *Impact and Influence*, the interviewer will be listening for/looking at whether you are good at reading people and are able to sell ideas effectively without overselling.		
To be successful in an interview, you need to: • Dress appropriately. • Behave appropriately. • Maintain good eye contact. • Have a good handshake. • Use the right gestures. • Smile at appropriate times. • Respect your interviewer's personal space. • Respond to your interviewer's nonverbal communication.		

Key Questions and Tasks	Reference Page	Complete
• Avoid giving a mixed message (where your nonverbal communication contradicts your words). • Deliver your news in an organized way. • Talk with your interviewer conversationally. Remember also to speak clearly and put some energy into your voice. Make sure that your interviewer can hear you, but be careful not to talk too loudly.		
Nonverbal cues change with the country and the culture in which you are interviewing. Before you interview in a country other than your own, research the common customs and business practices to understand what nonverbal communication may be important in an interview.		
Honesty is, of course, essential in any interview. However, there is a clear difference between being brutally honest and being diplimatically honest. Always try to put the best possible spin on your words while still being honest.		
When your nonverbal communication contradicts your verbal communication, the interviewer will believe the nonverbal message. To do well in an interview, avoid giving these "mixed messages."		
Always look your best the day of the interview. Try to lose some weight, if that will help you look and feel better. Buy a new suit, shoes, or tie, and get a haircut if you need one. If you need advice on your appearance, ask the most polished professional person you know for advice.		

Step 7: Remember Other Interview Tips

Key Questions and Tasks	Reference Page	Complete
When you think you are ready, do a little more preparation.		
Be prepared to respond, with competency-based answers, to four common interview questions: 1. Why are you interested in this position? *Focus on how your experience, competencies, and interests match the organization's needs.* 2. Tell me about yourself. *Focus on your work experience, highlighting evidence of the competencies for your target position.* 3. What are your strengths? *Focus on three or four of the competencies that are most important to the employer.* 4. What is your biggest weakness? *Focus on a weakness that does not relate to a critical component for the position. Be diplomatically honest. You may want to mention a weakness that might already be obvious from your interview (for example, not being as concise as possible).*		
Be prepared to discuss your "competency gaps"—competencies that you cannot prove, do not have, or that are not strengths for you. Talk about how you may have compensated for the gap by using your strength in another competency, or what you have done or plan to do to build strength in the competency.		

Key Questions and Tasks	Reference Page	Complete
Understand some basic truths about interviewing: • The best-qualified candidate does *not* always get the job. • Schedule interviews for the jobs you are more interested in *after* you've had a few "practice" interviews on jobs that you are less interested in. • The first few minutes of the interview *are* the most important. • Take a planner or notepad to the interview, but don't use it during the interview. Use it afterward to jot some notes to use in your thank-you notes. • Plan to arrive about 5 minutes early to an interview. If you arrive any earlier, you may be inconveniencing the interviewer, who has her own schedule to keep. • When responding to the question "Tell me about yourself," keep your answer to about 2 minutes. • Maintain good eye contact during the interview—but don't stare. • If asked about your previous or current supervisors or employers, be diplomatically honest, and do not talk negatively about them. • If the interviewer asks an illegal question, you must still respond, but try to determine the underlying reason for the question before giving your answer. Then give a diplomatic answer that responds to the underlying business need.		

Key Questions and Tasks	Reference Page	Complete
• Be as clear as possible in your answers and your nonverbal communication, because the interviewer's perceptions are the basis for determining who will be hired. • Make your work performance look as good as possible, and don't lie. • Your only job in the interview is to sell yourself, which leads to the next point:		

Preparing for the interview is the best use of your time, if you want to be perceived as a serious candidate for the job.

Chapter 9

Look at Case Studies for Ideas to Make Your Interviewing Stronger

When nothing seems to help, I go and look at a stonecutter
hammering away at his rock perhaps a hundred times
without as much as a crack showing in it.
Yet at the hundred and first blow it will split in two,
and I know it was not that blow that did it,
but all that had gone before.
—Jacob August Riis
photographer and author (1849–1914)

Although we're showing you a new way to get ready for interviews in this book, there are important lessons that you can learn from other people's experience with competency-based interviews. Read through the case studies included in this chapter and look for examples that remind you of some of your own problems or concerns.

The case studies were carefully chosen to give you an opportunity to see how we addressed some sticky issues when coaching these candidates to help them get ready for their interviews—competency-based interviews and more traditional interviews. Many of us have some things in our background that are difficult to explain in an interview and may get us in trouble with the interviewer. By looking at the case studies, you will see examples of how we addressed some issues that make the candidate's weak areas less obvious.

I believe you are a star, but I know that you may need to be reminded of that fact. You need to feel good about your own competence to do well in the interview. You may have just worked for a manager with a different personality than yours who did not see your strengths.

At one point in my own career, I worked for a human resources manager who told me I was a terrible writer! His style was simply different than mine—he believed in starting memos with phrases such as "Attached please find...."

You need to show the interviewer how strong you really are before, during, and after the interview. You can do this.

We'll show you what the issues were for four candidates and what solutions we developed.

Meet Jessica Gramm, a lawyer working for a prestigious law firm, who wants to work as a corporate attorney; Jack Blocker, a human resources vice president who lost his job; Dan Marrs, an information technology manager who wants a promotion within his current company; and Michael Blakeley, a college senior looking for his first job.

All of them have potential, and all of them have some issues that might cause an interviewer to choose someone else after the interview. You might have some similar things in your background. In these case studies, look at the ways these candidates learned to improve their change of getting what they wanted.

Case Study: Attorney

Situation

Jessica Gramm had worked as a litigation attorney for two major New York and Texas law firms, and specialized in handling general litigation and toxic torte cases. She had graduated near the top of her class at a nationally recognized law school in the South and had eight years of experience. She told me she wanted to work as an in-house counsel with a chemical or oil and gas company. Jessica recognized the benefits of working in-house:

- More collaboration and less direct competition with other attorneys.

- The chance to do more preventive work by offering good advice and training managers.

- Less emphasis on marketing, billing hours, and bringing in new clients.

- No concern about making partner.

When I met her, she told me that she had tried for the last two years to make the transition from working as an associate at a law firm to in-house counsel. Although she had interviewed with a few companies, she had not received any offers.

Action

I first worked closely with Jessica to develop a competency-based resume to replace her standard, more traditional resume. Like many lawyers, she was using a resume that covered her credentials, class standing, and the basic facts without giving many details of her accomplishments. We first analyzed an advertisement for a position as a staff attorney for one of the major oil and gas companies that uses competencies to help manage their human resources. We determined the key competencies for the position would have to include:

1. Achieves Results

2. Impact and Influence

3. Customer Service

4. Analytical Skills

5. Strategic Agility

6. Team Orientation

Then, I asked her to think about these competencies and give me an example of a time that she had done high-level work in each competency area. Jessica, who had always been a good student, took her homework assignment seriously and had her examples ready for the next time we met.

We worked together to develop effective accomplishment statements for her resume, targeting the key competencies. Here's an example of three of the accomplishment statements we used:

- Argued and won two Chapter 95 motions for summary judgment in torte cases with pipefitter and insulator as plaintiffs in front of state district judge, 2003–2004. (*Results*)

- Persuaded partner acting as first chair in trial to avoid using witness who demonstrated memory problems and became increasingly nervous on day before scheduled testimony. (*Influence*)

- Ensured credibility of human resources professional as witness by taking her through direct questions and mock cross-examination to help her know what to expect; recognized for contributing to successful verdict by supporting witness who had considerable difficulty in previous trial. (*Results and Customer Service*)

Once we had developed credible, targeted accomplishment statements, we worked on her summary section and completed the resume.

Within one week, Jessica called to let me know that she had been scheduled for an interview for the staff attorney position with the major oil and gas company. She recognized that the types of interviews done at law firms were very different than the interviews she had been through in corporations, and she knew she had not received the offer in the past. It was clearly time to try a different approach.

I knew the company she was interested in worked with competencies, and I told her to expect a typical competency-based interview using behavioral questions targeting those competencies. Some of the work we'd done getting the resume pulled together helped give her the background to more easily understand the competency-based approach to interviewing. So we went through a series of questions targeting the six key competencies we'd identified. I asked her to give me a few examples of times that she:

- Achieved positive results.

- Persuaded someone to do something that benefited the client.

- Went out of her way to help a client.

- Used her analytical skills to benefit her client.

- Developed a good legal strategy.

- Worked well with a team of people.

Like many lawyers, Jessica is articulate, but she had to polish her style to answer these kinds of questions well. She tended to give very general answers and seemed guarded about what she would share. Many lawyers tend to consider their work very confidential, but when they refuse to provide details, interviewers will perceive them as less credible.

So the key for the interviewee is to figure out cases and details that can be discussed, such as cases that are public record or no longer sensitive. I coached her to be more specific and to give the information necessary to provide evidence to the interviewers that she was strong in the competencies needed to be successful in the staff attorney role. I also explained how important it is to make sure to include the basics (discussed in Chapter 3) in every answer:

- What the situation or problem was.

- The action that you took.

- The result. (How did it benefit the organization or client?)

Result: Jessica did well on her first interview after we met and received an offer. Even with coaching, it is unusual for someone to do well on their first interview—so she did great! Most of us need more practice. She started at the major oil and gas company in January 2006. She called after her interview to tell me that the interviewers had asked these questions:

- Tell me about a time where you used your judgment to persuade a partner or senior manager to make a different decision in a case.

- Tell me about a time you used complex litigation analysis in a case. What was the result?

- Have you used a litigation strategy? Describe a case where you used a litigation strategy to help you manage the case, and tell us the steps you went through to determine the right litigation strategy to use. What happened?

- Tell us about a time you had to deal with a difficult issue with an employee. How did you handle it? What happened?

- Describe a situation where you had to deal with a difficult client. How did you handle the situation?

- Tell us about a time when you used your skills and knowledge to help the team. What was your role? What was the outcome or result of your input?

See if you can figure out which competencies the interviewers targeted with each questions. Look at Appendix B for my opinion.

Case Study: Human Resources Vice President

Situation

Jack Blocker had worked as a human resources vice president for two medium-sized manufacturing companies and had 30 years of human resources experience. Though he had gained some very good experience in his last role, Jack knew he was a little out of practice with interviewing—or at least doing well in his interviews. His last company had just been acquired by a competitor, and Jack had been doing some consulting work and looking for his next opportunity for about six months when we met.

He had a B.B.A. from the University of Michigan and had completed an M.B.A. two years earlier through the University of Phoenix online program. It was very clear Jack was angry about being without a job. He told me, "In all the years I've been working, I've never been treated the way I was by that last CEO."

Action

The first thing Jack and I spent some time talking about was his anger and frustration. I made the decision that Jack could handle my comment: "I think you're lucky. Most people can't say that they've worked 30 years and never been treated badly." He understood my point, thanked me, and told me that he knew I was right.

As a candidate, if you are angry, it will come across to the interviewer, and it will hurt your chance of being chosen for the position. Even if you think you are smart enough not to show your anger to the interviewer, it will probably still come across in the interview. Before you try to do well in your interviews, you need to do everything you can to resolve the anger—even meet with a mental health professional to get some help in this area.

Even though Jack had worked in human resources, he had worked for companies that were not leading-edge. His last company did not use competency-based interviewing, so when we first started talking about it, he recognized he had a few things to learn. He had read about competencies and had been trained on how to use behavioral interviewing. He recognized that in today's job market, he needed to know how to prepare for a competency-based interview for opportunities at all types of organizations.

We looked at some online advertisements and talked about what it takes to be successful in the top human resources position in an organization. Jack decided to focus his preparation around these competencies:

- Achieves Results

- Influence

- Customer Focus

- Building Business Partnerships, Relationships, and Teams

- Consulting

- Organizational Awareness, Agility, and Savvy

- Providing Feedback

- Understanding Business Goals

- Human Resources Expertise

Result

Jack decided to work through some of his anger with a mental health professional. Two months later, he worked with me to get ready for his interview. By that time, he had a more positive, can-do attitude, and was not going to be perceived as a victim using victim language. He was talking in a way that showed he was taking responsibility for the things that had happened. *Note: It is perfectly normal to be angry that things didn't work out with an employer, but you can't allow yourself the luxury of staying angry—particularly if you expect another employer to hire you. Just as Jack did, you need to deal with the issues and get over being angry before you can really move on.*

Jack went on several interviews over the next three or four months, and did not limit his job search to manufacturing companies, even though that was his background. He was eventually given a job offer to be the Director of Human Resources at a medium-sized government contractor in the Washington, D.C. metropolitan area. In professional areas such as human resources, it is often easier to change industries—as Jack did—because a large part of the technical work stays the same, but you will always have an edge if you have experience with that same industry.

During his interview at the government contractor, the CEO and president of the company asked Jack these questions:

- Describe a time that you had to work especially hard to get a good result. What did you do?

- Tell us about a time that you had to influence a group of people to be able to lead them effectively.

- When you first started with your current employer, what did you do to learn the specific things about the industry that you needed to know to be effective in human resources? How did you decide what was especially important?

- Tell us about one of the most effective business partnerships you've been involved in building. What did you do to help make it so effective? Did you have to overcome any obstacles? Describe what happened.

- Have you been involved with introducing any new ideas or programs into your organization? Tell us about the program, and describe the steps you used to improve the acceptance for the program.

- Tell us about a time you made a mistake. What did you learn from it?

Case Study: Director, Information Technology

Situation

Dan Marrs was an information technology product development manager working for American Express in St. Louis. I first met him two years ago when he became the first person from a competency-based organization to ask me to help him develop a competency-based resume. At the time, I was in the early stages of writing *Competency-Based Resumes*.

Dan wanted to stay with American Express—and he also wanted a promotion. He knew that a competency-based resume targeting the key competencies for promotional opportunities would help improve the likelihood he would be selected for an interview. He came to me with a list of competencies[1] for the positions within American Express he wanted to post for:

- Creates Innovative Solutions

- Thinks Analytically

- Acts Strategically and Globally

- Drives Results

- Exceeds Customer Expectations

- Risk-Taking

- Acts Decisively

- Collaborates and Influences Others

- Demonstrates Integrity

- Treats People with Respect

- Manages Performance

- Develops People

- Manages Change

(The competency-based resume that we developed together is on pages 46 and 47 in the book *Competency-Based Resumes*.) Dan used the competency-based resume to apply for a few positions within the company.

Action

Dan knew that even though he was a strong candidate, other American Express candidates would also be well-qualified for the positions he was interested in. He knew he could not take anything for granted. When an interview was scheduled, he called for help to be as prepared as possible.

We focused on the list of competencies he knew were important to be successful in the position he was going to be interviewing for. Candidates who have written a competency-based resume will have an easier time getting ready for a competency-based interview because they have already spent time thinking about what they have done to prove they are strong in each competency area.

So I first asked Dan to think of his accomplishments in each competency—and have two or three examples in each area. I reminded him that he needed to be able to explain the situation or problem, the action he took, and the result of the action—the benefit to the team or the organization. I listened to his answers and coached him to be:

- Strategic with the examples he picked.

- Concise and powerful with the language he used.

- Professional and approachable with his nonverbal communication.

Result

He interviewed, did well, and received the promotion about a year ago.

In most cases, candidates do better in their second or third interviews than in their first one. The first interview any candidate has after a long period of time without interviewing helps get the candidate ready for other interviews. Dan interviewed first for another position within the company and was almost selected.

When he found out that another candidate had been chosen, he talked to the key managers and asked, confidentially, for suggestions about what he could do to improve as a candidate. They told him that he wasn't chosen for the position because he didn't have experience managing more than one person and that the other candidate had that experience. Dan *had* managed a group of six employees—*but it was before he worked for American Express*. Instead of arguing the point, Dan took steps to officially mentor employees and actively looked for opportunities to manage teams within American Express. He stayed professional and kept working hard.

Dan also received feedback that the interviewers evaluated him primarily on what he said during the interview. He had worked directly with most of the interview team and felt comfortable that they knew what he had done and what he was capable of doing in the future. So Dan, in his first interview, had not provided the interview team with certain examples that showcased his competencies particularly well because he assumed they knew his work on those projects.

Before his second interview, Dan prepared by thinking about the critical competencies for the position—as he had done for the first opportunity. In addition, he made a conscious effort to answer the competency-based behavioral questions in the interview with his best, highest-level examples and to explain them well. He was not going to make the mistake again of assuming his interviewers would be able to consider examples he did not directly address. On several of the questions, he said he just "spoke as if the interviewers didn't know me."

Here are a few of the questions he was asked:

- Tell us about a situation where you had to take several actions over a period of time and overcome obstacles in order to achieve a business objective.

- Describe a time when you had to identify some key issues in order to guide a group toward the right decision.

- Think of a time when you had many challenging projects with different priorities to manage. Tell us about it.

Managers at companies like American Express are usually given follow-up questions to help them probe for additional information. Dan knew he could expect follow-up questions, so he had reviewed his background and was prepared to talk about any statistic or detail of a project he used as an example.

Dan was ready to be promoted, and he'd shown his willingness to do what he could to develop his background. He learned from the feedback he had been given, and he thought seriously about his competencies before the next interview. Without a doubt, Dan was prepared for his next interview, and obviously he did well. He received his promotion and is now a director in information technology at American Express.

Case Study: College Graduate, Engineering

Situation

Michael Blakeley graduated in December 2005 with a B.S. in Electrical Engineering from the University of Illinois, with an additional six classes in Computer Engineering. He had studied hard and had a 3.57 GPA in a tough engineering program. Like many college students, Michael thought he should focus on his classes and get good grades. He did not think working as an engineering co-op or during the summers was that important. So, during his four years in college, he had only worked one summer for a small manufacturing plant in a Chicago suburb. Michael had signed up for several on-campus interviews during the fall semester and had discovered that his limited work experience made him less likely to get selected for interviews than his classmates who had participated in the school's engineering co-op program or had worked in the summer engineering intern programs run by Fortune 500 companies.

Action

When I began working with him, he was getting discouraged. Michael had learned the hard way that having good work experience, through formal internships or co-op programs—or simply summer jobs—makes a difference with employers. I agreed—he *should* have more solid work experience at this point—but it was too late to encourage him to get that experience during his last semester in college.

I talked with him and discovered that, even though he had not done the formal engineering internships or co-op program, he *had* worked to set up, program, and maintain computers for small businesses, individuals, and nonprofit organizations.

We worked together to rewrite his resume—the competency-based way. I asked him questions about times that he'd demonstrated his competencies in these areas:

- Achieved good results

- Showed initiative

- Used his analytical skills

We looked at some online advertisements to see which other competencies companies were looking for in entry-level engineering training programs and other positions. We decided to add:

- Customer Service

- Engineering and Computer Competencies

- Planning and Organizing

- Information-seeking

Working with these seven competencies, I was able to help him develop a much more impressive competency-based functional resume that included some strong accomplishments that his more traditional resume had not included. Some examples? He had:

- Worked on a team that won the best engineering project in the electrical engineering department his senior year.

- Developed a solution to a particularly difficult virus on the computer network for a nonprofit organization working with unemployed people in St. Louis, Missouri.

I encouraged him to continue working with his college placement office—but to also start doing a competency-based job search on his own.

Before he could actively start a more complete search, he received an offer with a medium-sized manufacturing company that his uncle worked for. The human resources manager offered him a contract engineering position at one of their plants for a six-month period. He took the offer even though I encouraged him to keep looking for a full-time, regular position with benefits with a company offering a good training program. Two weeks later, a larger manufacturer announced they planned to acquire the company that had given him the offer.

Right before Christmas, Michael was told that the company was going to have to rescind his offer. Michael knew when he called me that it was time to do a much more thorough job search. With his graduation behind him, Michael no longer had the *distraction* of maintaining a good GPA to keep him from focusing on looking for a job.

When I talked with him in early January, we started working on a list of target companies and organizations for Michael. In less than one hour, we had 30 companies on his list. It is important to look at this kind of list as a work-in-progress and try to be aware of organizations that could be added to this list.

When we put together his list, Michael told me that he'd visited the human resources manager for one of those companies in the hospital with one of his volunteer groups at school. He also knew key managers at five of the targeted organizations because they were family friends or, in one case, the mother of one of his own friends. And I had contacts for him at four more of the companies. So Michael, without thinking that hard, had connections at 10 of the organizations he thought he'd be interested in working for. I gave him some ideas about what to say when he talked to his contacts and how to word e-mails and cover letters so that they would be more competency-based.

In addition, Michael still had access to his college placement office and could sign up for interviews during the spring semester. I coached him to go through the list from the school and take advantage of any help the school could offer him. The other thing Michael agreed to do during the next week was to make sure he was listed on Monster.com, CareerBuilder.com, and Dice.com, which is a site focused on technical professions. He also agreed to check these job sites at least twice each week to see if they had any opportunities he wanted to apply for.

Result

By the end of January, Michael had been on three interviews and was waiting to see if he was going to get an offer.

The interviewers asked him competency-based interview questions including:

1.   Tell me about an assignment in school or at work where you needed to have strong analytical skills to do well.

    •   How did you plan and organize the work?

    •   How did you decide what information you would need?

2.   Have you worked with a difficult customer? Describe what happened.

3. Tell me about the most difficult engineering or computer project you've worked on. Describe what obstacles you ran into, and tell me how you overcame them.

Michael is a very good candidate and has much stronger interpersonal skills than most of the engineering students in their early 20s that I've met in the last few years. In fact, he is very likeable, and one recruiter who met him described him to me as "charming." He's also a good, conscientious student and has proven to me that he's willing to take the job search project seriously and work hard at it. So I have every confidence that, as you read this book, Michael will be working at a company where his supervisor is beginning to realize she hired a very good employee.

Chapter 10

Understand How a Typical Competency-Based Interview Flows

In the book *Blink: The Power of Thinking Without Thinking* (Little, Brown, 2005), author Malcolm Gladwell makes this point: "We learn by example and by direct experience because there are real limits to the adequacy of verbal instruction."

In this chapter, I'm going to take Malcolm Gladwell's advice and give you an example to show you the way a competency-based interview flows—from start to finish. After all, an interview is a conversation between the interviewer and you. Or, more and more often these days, it may be a conversation between a group of people and you. To do well, you need to recognize what is happening during the interview.

Most typical interviews last 30 to 40 minutes, unless you are interviewing for a more senior position in an organization. And many organizations still conduct several individual interviews with candidates, one interviewer after another. The other major exception to the timing is when you are being interviewed by a panel or team; these interviews typically are longer and are being used more frequently.

Most interviews can be broken into three parts: the introduction, the body, and the conclusion.

We'll be talking about each of these and I'll give you some specific examples to give you a better understanding of the basic interview flow.

> *It is important to realize as a candidate, though, that interviewers have different levels of competence at conducting interviews and assessing candidates.*

Interview—Introduction

Typically, at the beginning of the interview, the interviewer will meet you in the lobby, introduce himself, shake your hand, and walk with you to the office or conference room. Review the suggestions in Chapter 6 for how you can be perceived as a strong candidate from the very beginning of the interview based on your nonverbal communication skills. Remember how critical it is to make a good first impression.

Although every organization may interview a little differently, it is not unusual for the interviewer to ask an *icebreaker* type of question at the beginning, such as:

- Did you have any difficulty finding the office?

- What do you think of the area?

- Do you want any water or coffee?

If you need to sign any forms, take any career tests, or complete any applications, you will probably be asked to do these things when you first arrive or when the interviewer first meets you.

The interviewer may start the interview by confirming some things in your background. You may even be asked some questions about degrees, dates, past employers from your resume or application—just to confirm details or clarify anything that may not be clear to the interviewer. The interviewer may also tell you about the organization's interview process and who you are scheduled to talk with that day.

Interview—Body

In the body of a competency-based interview, the interviewer asks behavioral questions structured to help the interviewer determine how strong the candidate is in the competencies critical for success in the position.

To help you see how this works, I've included one interview example in this chapter: a financial sales professional looking for another opportunity. After every answer to an interview question, I've included some coaching tips to help you understand how the answers could be stronger. Because we can't see some of the nonverbal communication in these examples, the coaching tips are limited to the answers themselves. The next chapter will give you the opportunity to learn from three other professionals: an IT project manager, a consultant, and a financial analyst.

Read through these interview segments carefully. Look for responses that the candidates give that you think work well for them, and where they could improve. Think about how you would respond to these questions yourself. Then review the coaching tips. Hopefully, you will get some ideas about what you can say and do to make your next interview more positive and productive.

Each interviewee is a good candidate, and as an interviewer, I'd be happy hiring any of them. They have different strengths as interviewees and different things to work on to learn to be more effective.

My advice? Read through these examples to get additional tips on what you can do to *nail* the next interview.

Financial Sales Professional

Can you tell me about a project that had a pending deadline that you have worked on and what obstacles you encountered?

When I was at Beneficial, I worked on an automated solicitation campaign project. The purpose was to develop an automated system to send out solicitation offers to existing customers. The team had three months to design, test, and implement the system. Time was the biggest obstacle that we had to overcome. The team consisted of branch mangers and assistant mangers who did not want to spend a lot of time away from their offices. Another problem was getting the staff of the branches to buy into the automated system.

Coaching

- Overall, good answer.
- This answer would be stronger if you *directly* addressed the underlying question about your results. Did your team get the project done by the deadline? Did your management recognize you for completing the project on time or under budget, or for the high quality of the work? What was the bottom-line result of the project?
- Whenever you answer this type of question, expect to get a follow-up question if you don't address the obvious question about how you overcame the hurdles in your first answer.

How did you overcome these obstacles?

I developed a weekly assignment calendar. Each team member was responsible for completing his task each week. We would have a conference call once every two weeks and meet twice a month. This system allowed the managers to be able to stay in their offices. In order to get the staff to buy into the system each manager would ask for input from his or her most senior staff member about the design of the solicitation pieces, and we would share with our staffs how the system would look and work so that the staff felt that there were part of the project.

Coaching

- Good details. This answer would be stronger, though, if you'd summarized your main points in more of a topic sentence at the beginning of your statement. Here's an example of a good way to begin your answer to the question about how you overcame the obstacles: "By making every effort to make sure our team communicated effectively and understood their assignments and goals."

- Good point about getting the staff buy in. You showed you understood how to motivate the team by bringing that up.

- Clarify your own role. Were you one of the managers or a senior staff member? Your answer doesn't make this clear.

What was your role in the project?

To make sure that we stayed on task and the project was completed on time. I also helped with the design of the solicitation pieces.

Coaching

- This answer needs more of an explanation, especially if it was asked before the last question.

- More details would help make your role clearer. Did you coordinate the conference calls?

Can you think of a time when you were below your sales goal during the middle of the month or missed a sales goal? What did you do to improve your numbers?

When I worked as a financial advisor for Fidelity, we were in the middle of an intra-office contest, and I was about 10 percent below my goal, and the contest was ending in about 14 business days. I went through my client list and reviewed previous financial plans to see which clients were due for their yearly reviews or if there were parts of the plan that needed to be implemented. I stayed late each night and contacted each client to schedule review appointments. If my client could not make an appointment I asked for a referral that I might be able to contact to schedule for a financial planning session. Using this method allowed me to get my production back on track, and I finished the contest in the top five.

Coaching

- Very good logical answer with some details and specifics to make your answer credible.

- Remember that your answers need to be conversational, and the first part of your answer is just too long. Take a breath! Use shorter sentences to avoid dominating the conversation or just boring the interviewer.

- Give more details to support how hard you worked to make the goal. How many clients were on your list? How late did you stay each night? 9 p.m.? Keep in mind that what is late for one person does not always seem late to another.

Tell me about why you have been successful in sales.

I develop a relationship with my clients built on trust and respect. I try to work with my clients using a team approach so that they feel that I have their best interests at heart.

Coaching

- Good introduction, but you need to support your answer with some specific examples of when you have developed client relationships in the past, at former employers such as American Express and Fidelity. You will build your own credibility with the interviewer by citing clients who have referred business to you or given a larger percentage of their overall net worth to you to manage. Remember that most interviewers are taught that past behavior is the best predictor of future behavior. So by giving examples of when you have developed productive relationships in the past, you are providing evidence you will be able to develop them in the future.

Interview—Conclusion

After the interviewer has completed asking the competency-based behavioral interview questions that are included in his interview guide, he will probably ask you if you have any questions for him. If you don't ask questions, the interviewer will simply perceive you as not being that interested in the position. You should *always* have some questions to ask.

So what are good questions to ask the interviewer?

1. Questions that demonstrate a genuine interest in the work. The interviewer is talking to you because he needs help doing the work.
2. Questions that demonstrate you were listening during the interview.

Ask questions such as these:

- When you think about the other people you've seen working in this position, would you tell me about the employee that you think has been the most successful? What did she do in her first year (or six months) to help her be so successful?

  (*Note: Pay attention to the answer. It can give you very good information about what the manager is looking for in a good employee.*)

- What are your goals for the department? Tell me about them, and why they are important to the organization.

- Tell me about how you have the work divided in the department.

- When you were talking a little earlier, you mentioned that:

  - Example 1: The company planned to acquire another company in the next year or two.

  - Example 2: The organization was starting to work with competencies.

  - Example 3: The department was getting some new technology applications soon.

  (*Note: Follow up any of these examples by asking the interviewer to tell you more about it.*)

You may be thinking that these questions look quite similar to the behavioral interviewing questions that you've been learning about throughout this book. Congratulations. You're thinking as a good, highly competent professional now. The reasons you should ask these kinds of questions are:

- They help demonstrate that you want the position and are willing to learn from your future manager.

- They give the manager an opportunity to talk and give you some good information that may help you understand the position, the coworkers, the manager, and the organization's culture better.

- They show the interviewer that you are smart, current, and savvy, in a good way.

After you have asked a few questions, see if the interviewer takes back the control of the interview. If he doesn't, you might want to tell him, "I know I could keep talking with you for a long time because I think this opportunity is really interesting, and I'm having a good time talking with you, but I'm sure you have some other important things that you need to do." See what he says. When one client used this approach during a second interview with a powerful senior vice president at the company, he looked at her, smiled, and said, "Okay, you can ask me two more questions." So she did, and she received a job offer three hours later.

Usually, interviewers will tell you what to expect next before you leave the interview. If your interviewer doesn't volunteer this information, tell him that you've been very impressed with everyone you've met and are even more interested in the position than you were before the interview. Ask the question, "What's the next step?" in a nice, professional way.

And make sure you have contact information for every interviewer. The easiest way to get their names, e-mails, mailing addresses, and phone numbers is to ask for their business cards if they don't automatically give one to you.

When you leave, make sure to write down some notes about what was said during the interview. Try to do this when you get to your car or when you get home that day. You'll need the notes to write targeted, competency-based thank-you notes to the interviewers.

Chapter 11

Learn From Other Interviewees

In the last chapter, you learned about the way a fairly typical competency-based interview flows. You read the answers given by a financial sales professional to some competency-based interview questions and had the opportunity to learn from the coaching comments.

Confucius said, "By three methods we may learn wisdom: First by reflection, which is noblest; second, by imitation, which is easiest; and third, by experience, which is bitterest." In this chapter, you're going to be able to gain some wisdom from the interview experience of three real people: an IT project manager, a compensation and benefits consultant, and a financial analyst.

The examples included in this chapter specifically do not include the introductions or concluding parts of the interview to make it easier for you to focus on the types of questions that are included in typical competency-based interviews. The answers the candidates gave were not perfect—few answers are ever perfect. So to give you some idea of how the answers could be better, I've included coaching comments.

Read through these questions and answers carefully. Look for examples that you can relate to. Take some notes and notice if an answer, part of an answer, or a coaching comment helps trigger an idea for how you might give a better answer in your next interview. Remember that our goal is not perfection, but, to paraphrase Confucius, to gain wisdom. At least about interviewing.

IT Project Manager, Interviewing for Another Opportunity Within His Company

Tell me about a time when you led a team to complete a project. Give an example of a challenge that significantly impacted the project, and describe how you resolved the issue.

The project was to lead a team of 10 people to complete installation of new software for Website access to client data. The challenge was the team consisted of 10 people but several were contract offshore technical resources that were partially allocated to my project and were only dotted-line reporting to me. What made the situation even more difficult were the time differences between Bangalore, India, and the Ft. Lauderdale office, the language differences, and not being trained on the new software.

What I did to mitigate the issues was to pair the contact individuals with a U.S. counterpart. I set up a buddy system to complete specific project task items. The U.S. member was responsible to support the contract partner with needed information or obtain a trained person to support completing the task. Specific weekly conference calls in the evening in the United States to coincide with India's next-day morning were scheduled to track the progress and identify solutions for outstanding issues. Items that required more time to complete that impacted the time line were communicated to management as a risk.

Coaching

- Basically, good answer with enough details to make the example credible.

- If you realize that one of the most important competencies targeted with this question is *achieve results*, you need to focus more on the project results to make this answer even stronger. This is a good example of why understanding the purpose of a competency-based interview can make a huge difference in the quality of your answer.

- Make sure you use conversational language. Most of us rarely use words like *mitigate* or *obtain* when we talk—we might say *manage the issues* or *get* instead. However, if the organization you are interviewing with *does* commonly use these specific words in conversation, go ahead and use them.

- Take credit for the steps you took to lead the project. Who decided to schedule the weekly calls? Who actually scheduled them?

- Use more active language to describe your role. Who communicated the items that took more time to management? Avoid using passive language.

Give an example of when you had to deliver bad news. Tell how you delivered it and what the response was.

The situation was the delivery of an enhancement to a large database share by multiple systems without interrupting current operations. The enhancement would facilitate down-line reporting to a business unit that is not an owner of the database. This project is an exception to provide data that would generate $1 million in incremental revenue for the company. The bad news was a higher priority project for the database owners was approved without considering it would delay the "outside" project by a forecasted three months. I had to deliver the news to unreceptive senior management sponsors. I immediately communicated a summary of the "potential" delay, and what I had done to address the risk. I deliberately said "potential" to communicate the risk without alarming the project sponsors by giving too many details. I immediately escalated to my senior management to advise them of the risk. I also suggested a compromise solution to blend the two projects as an option for my senior management. After negotiation between senior management sponsors, the solution was accepted. The actions of immediate escalation and providing a solution for my management to offer were key to implementing a prompt solution and prevented a major conflict.

Coaching

- Some good information in this answer, but it needs to be more concise and conversational.

- Use active language to describe the situation, action, and result. Say, "I was told by my manager that a higher priority project had been approved that would cause a delay in several areas—including the project I was working on."

- Try to be consistent with the tenses you use when you are giving your answers.

- Be specific. How many senior management sponsors did you deliver the news to?

- Take credit for the things that you have done and be clear about who did what. Who negotiated between senior management sponsors? Did you take the actions of immediately communicating with your senior management and providing a solution? If so, make that clear when you are giving your answer!

Tell us about a time when you demonstrated your ability to effectively communicate to a group. Describe the situation and explain how you knew if you got your message across.

There is an annual company Tech Conference where more than a thousand clients attend. My responsibility was to present a Management Information product session. The presentation intent was to convey a reporting product is simple and flexible enough to support individual users while sophisticated enough to provide global report consolidation. What made it successful was focusing on the benefits of the core product and value to audience via the use of samples of real situations and conducted the session from the value to the audience perspective. In the presentation I overlaid the power of reporting over the true power of the data with comparisons to alternative options. I focused on data management and assumptions—not on the tool. The presentation also included data flow charts and report samples. My presentation received the highest rating out of 50 sessions in the conference via attendee surveys. Not only is this presentation style successful for conference clients, but also with internal peers and colleagues in training sessions.

Coaching

- Be more concise and conversational. This whole answer is too wordy.

- Make sure you identify details such as when the event happened.

- The first two sentences would be more effective if reduced to one statement such as, "I was asked to present a Management Information product session at the company's 2004 Tech Conference." It is probably reasonable to assume that, because this interview is for another position within your company, the interviewers would know about the size of the conference and how important it is to the company.

- Use more active language, such as "I knew that the presentation needed to get across how easy the product is to use for individuals while being sophisticated enough to provide global report consolidations."

- Talk about your result—getting the highest rating at the conference—earlier. That's the most impressive and important part of your answer, and talking about it as your second sentence would give it the emphasis it deserves.

- Good conclusion, but it would be stronger if you phrased it so that it shows what you learned from working on and delivering the presentation. Start the sentence with "I learned that...."

Provide an occasion when you made a sound decision even though you didn't have as much information as you would have liked.

I was managing a project integrating new software that had not been implanted anywhere in the company. There was no experience with installing. The vendor had no experience with how our company wanted to configure and utilize the features. By the second milestone, it became clear the installation would not be completed in one year, and I would need to ask for additional time and funding to complete the project. Given the urgency to migrate from the old system to the new, senior management needed to understand what the real estimate would be before authorizing the scope change. I asked the technology and servicing team to analyze and assess the phasing of the project. My recommendation was to use an unrelated but similar project as a baseline assumption, and my managers agreed. Once we completed a deep level of analysis, I was able to extrapolate a new time line and scope for the first year delivery with current funding and a reasonable level of risk. Additionally, I also presented the consequences of not continuing the project to better balance the investment decision. The outcome was that the phased project approach was accepted.

Coaching

- Basically, a good answer.
- Use more active language. For the second sentence, say, "No one in the company knew about installing the software." For the last sentence use, "The senior managers accepted my recommendation to phase the project in."

Describe how you handled a situation to make sure you stayed on track and completed the tasks needed to drive results.

The project was in response to an urgent senior executive request to complete a one-off development enhancement to the product for a high-visibility client to use. I was told I needed to complete the project without interrupting the work on any of my other projects. To be successful and meet my manager's needs, I reviewed the expected deliverables with the client. I needed to understand the detailed information about their needs to then use the information in providing an estimate. As estimates include time, cost, and scope, and talking with the client immediately helped me identify that I would need to reset expectations on the delivery time line. An expectation for an early delivery was improperly communicated to client. The requirements needed development of a new process design. I organized a team of subject matter experts and whittled the options down to the optimal option that could be incorporated into an existing project. Although there were numerous issues that required changes in design and subsequently project scope, the project was completed within the year without incremental cost to the client or the existing project the enhancement was incorporated into. Sharing existing resources was key in completing the enhancement. The key tool in contributing to timely delivery was my maintaining a project plan to identify resource availability and task prioritization.

Coaching

- Good example with enough details to be credible. Going through the steps you took, step by step, works well.

- Think through your entire answer and edit it to eliminate unnecessary words and details. Focus on what is critical for the interviewer to know to understand the example. This answer seems as though it would be a first draft in a paper—you need to be talking in final draft form to be really effective in the interview.

- Start your answer by explaining your role ("I was asked to be the project manager for…").

- Use more active—not passive—verbs.

- Take credit for the things you and the other people did on the project by being more direct in your statements.

- Avoid using words like *various* and *numerous* when you are answering questions. These words don't add anything to the content. You've already shown that there is more than one *issue* simply by adding an "s" and making it clear that you are talking about *issues*.

Consultant

Tell me about yourself.

I'm a problem-solver who thrives on new challenges, and I enjoy following a project through to completion and assessing the team's performance. I prefer working in a team and appreciate the opportunities to share my own ideas and learn from others. I am generally very quick to see connections between parts of a project, or between a project and the areas of the organization that it is intended to impact. I don't mind hard work and long hours, particularly if a project presents the chance to build my knowledge and skills.

Coaching

- Good answer to *part* of what you need to talk about, but you need to do a better job of answering the question of "Can you do the job?" covered in Chapter 3.

- It would be a definite plus for you to include, at the end of the answer to the question, a statement about what you want to do next and why you are ready to do it.

- Try to make your answer just a little more conversational, with shorter sentences and slightly more informal language.

- This answer would also be stronger if you led with your profession—"I'm a senior consultant."

- Unless you are confident that a position is 100 percent teamwork, avoid the possible perception that you can't work alone by adding the statement that you are also good working independently when you talk about teams.

- Avoid using neutral language such as you don't *mind* something because it can create the perception that you actually *do* have a problem with it.

Tell me about a time you felt particularly good about the results you were able to get on an assignment.

I worked with a partner on an assignment to revamp the salary and incentive compensation program for a major retailing conglomerate. Initially, we worked with two of their larger divisions, store chains based in Ohio and Texas. As their management watched our progress, and we shared our preliminary findings, they were so impressed that they asked us to extend the project timetable to incorporate four additional divisions. Ultimately, we also conducted an executive pay study with personnel at the corporate headquarters.

Coaching

- Overall, very good answer.

- This answer would be a little stronger if you started with the "bottom line"—a statement summarizing the basic answer. Here's an example: "I worked on a project for Home Depot, and they were so happy with the quality of work that the client added two new divisions to the project after the first month. That meant more than $250,000 in additional consulting fees for the firm."

- Be more specific. Give names of clients and details of projects, including size and scope. Quantify—with statistics and overall consulting fees whenever possible. (It is okay to estimate or round if you don't have the exact number. Take the time to go through your notes or call a former colleague to verify the information if possible.)

- Make sure that the language you use is conversational. The word *ultimately* is a little more formal than you need to be in an interview.

- Remember to stay current with the words you use. Use *employees* instead of *personnel*.

Tell me about a situation when you had to think outside the box to come up with a good solution.

We try to use published surveys to determine appropriate salary levels for organizations, but we've encountered some situations in which the data just doesn't exist. In working with a major telecommunications company, we found several unique jobs that were difficult to place in the company's hierarchy. To determine values for these jobs, we used two approaches. First, we worked with senior management and the managers of these positions to develop very clear job requirements and responsibilities, and we then were able to suggest comparable jobs in the company as well as in other industries. We also used our own sources, including clients, and asked our client contact to provide us with some sources, to obtain salary data at competitive organizations, with the agreement that we would share the data with any organization that contributed to the survey. Through these two avenues, we were able to get more accurate pictures of these jobs, both internally and externally, and client management felt that our results were very credible.

Coaching

- You need to explain why the two approaches you mentioned are really "outside the box." It is hard to tell from your answer. It would seem that most organizations would have some unique jobs, and your consulting group would have figured out a basic approach to use. So give more of an explanation here, and, if you can't, consider choosing a different example.

- Be careful about using the word *we* when talking about your work. Clarify your own role. Many interviewers would perceive that as showing that you still think of yourself as part of your past or current employer's team—and that you would have trouble making the transition to working for the new manager or employer.
- Make the answer more conversational. Use shorter sentences.

Have you managed a project where it was difficult to meet the deadline or stay within the budget?

Yes.

Tell us what happened. How did you address the situation?

We were hired to complete an incentive compensation study for a public utility. Although senior management was involved in the initial meeting, our major contact, the project manager, was at a lower level in the organization. The project manager was constantly trying to extend the scope of the project, asking us to do weekly reports and to cost out many more alternative scenarios than we normally produced. After almost a month of his requests, we asked our relationship manager to contact the senior managers for a progress meeting. When it became clear to the senior managers that we were doing much more than the planned work, they asked us to elaborate on the expected results of our efforts. The end result of the meeting was that the project scope was officially extended, with a revised budget and timetable, so that we could produce some of the additional requested studies and recommendations.

Coaching

- I suspect you missed an opportunity to show the interviewer some evidence of your organizational awareness and agility or interpersonal savvy competencies. Take the time to explain why you asked for a progress meeting. Did you ask for the meeting because you weren't sure the project manager was keeping her senior management informed? Or because you wanted to make sure that the executives wanted the expanded scope of the project—and would be willing to pay for it? Either reason shows the interviewer some good things about the way you think and handle yourself professionally.

Describe a time that you had to use your ability to influence a manager to be able to do a good job.

I was assigned, along with a project manager, to complete a relatively simple compensation study at a hospital. The project manager had asked to be assigned to a bigger, more-high-profile assignment that was given to another consultant in our group, so he was less than enthusiastic about our project. Once I realized the issue, he and I strategized about ways to complete the project under budget and ahead of schedule, while still maintaining the expected quality and client satisfaction levels. Although we ultimately spent the full budget, the work was completed two weeks ahead of schedule, and our group manager considered that performance in promoting my colleague to a unit manager, which happened about six months after we completed our project.

Coaching

- Very strong example. It not only shows good influencing skills, but you also are providing evidence of several other competencies, including achieving results and interpersonal skills.

- Be more specific—what is relatively simple to one person may not be simple to another.

- Use more conversational language, and be a little more concise. For example, in the last statement, say, "when he promoted my colleague to a unit manager six months later."

Tell us about a time you worked with a difficult person on your team.

One of our compensation consultants was well-known for his domineering style in managing projects. He insisted on leading every meeting with the clients and allowed the other team members to talk only rarely. At the same time, he required his team members to prepare all of the materials for each meeting, which he would critique quite candidly in front of the whole project team. In an attempt to help him recognize and change his style, the group managers assigned the two of us as coleaders of a project with a major aircraft manufacturer. He asked to be reassigned to another project, but the managers refused his request. When it became clear that we would need to work together closely, he gave me his opinion of how the project should be run, and it was clear that he expected me to just accept his ideas. Based on our conversation, I put together a timetable for the project, showing major activities and meetings. I then sat down with him and said that, though I agreed with his concept of how the project should be structured, I wanted to share more of the workload with him. Although it took a couple of sessions with my chart to get agreement on "sharing the load," we did reach what I considered to be an acceptable compromise to his original plan, and our managers were impressed that we both were able to modify our working styles to accommodate each other and our client.

Coaching

- Good choice for your answer. It demonstrates to the interviewer how strong your interpersonal skills are and your matter-of-fact, pragmatic approach to working with a difficult personality.

- It is critical to give an answer to this question. It is just not credible to say that you have never worked with someone difficult. But if you show anger, judgment, or another negative emotional response in your answers or in your nonverbal communication, the interviewer will perceive you negatively. Be careful. Pick an example showing your wisdom and professional approach to problem-solving.

- Be more conversational with the language you use, and work on being a little more concise and to the point. Ideally, you want to give your answers using final-draft language—without redundancies and extra words that don't add to the content.

Financial Analyst With Experience in Banking and Healthcare, Interviewing for Position With Major Hospital System

Tell me about your background.

I have 15 years experience in banking as a financial analyst and have worked for the last year in healthcare. Over the years, I have completed studies in banking departments that have included Process Reengineering and improving operating departments through streamlining processes. I've also most recently managed the Customer Profitability Reporting area, where I have focused on the profitability of our customers and ways to cross-sell and increase revenue.

Coaching

- Be careful not to emphasize the number of years of experience you have. As one manager explained, "Someone can have the same year of experience 15 times." This is especially important for those of us older than the age of 35 or 40 who may be concerned about age discrimination. The important thing to emphasize in your answer is your relevant experience: evidence to prove to the interviewer that you are competent in the key competency areas that are needed for someone to be successful in the position.

- Good job of explaining your overall background concisely. Typically, the answer to this question takes two minutes to present, so in my opinion, most interviewers would view this answer as being too brief.

- This answer would be stronger if you added an explanation of what has motivated you in the past, what your strengths are, what you want to do next, and why you want to do that type of work.

Tell me about a project you worked on where your analytical skills were critical.

As manager of the Customer Profitability Group at BankOne, I had to look at the profitability of the bank's customers and determine which customers were the most profitable and offered the most opportunity for future revenue growth. I also focused on customers with the least revenue potential and initiated exit strategies.

Coaching

- Be more conscious of using language that makes you sound positive. "I had to look at the profitability" could be perceived by the interviewer as if someone made you do that and that you were a victim. Fix the problem by saying, "I analyzed the profitability...."

- Give some numbers, statistics, dollars, or some other measurement to let the interviewer know the size of the project.

- This answer is okay, but it would be much stronger with more details. How many customers did you review? What process did you use to analyze the information? Did you set up a spreadsheet or database program to help you analyze the information?

- For a much better answer, tell the interviewer what your final recommendation to your manager was, and explain how the bank (or your department) benefited from the analytical work.

Think about a time when you had to put in extra effort to get the results you needed at work. Tell me about it.

This is an ongoing issue. I'm always going the extra mile. If I need to get a report deadline made, I will make it happen by initiating the result needed and making whatever calls I need to get all the pieces to the puzzle complete and on time.

Coaching

- Good general answer, but it would be much better if you brought it down to a specific example. In this case, after giving the general answer, add details such as, "Here's one recent example. Last week, my manager came to my office after lunch and asked me to step in and finish a report for a colleague who had to leave work early when she found out that her fifth grader had broken his leg in a soccer game. The report was due the next morning. I called my colleague on her cell phone, got the details from her, tracked down the information for the monthly report from key department heads, entered the data, and had the report finished and e-mailed to my manager by 8 p.m. that evening."

Have you dealt with some difficult clients or customers while working at the bank or hospital? Pick a situation and tell me about it.

Yes, there are always difficult customers, whether they are internal to the organization or external. One of the most successful strategies is to ask them about ways to improve processes and get their input. By including them in the discussion and valuing their input and finding out what you can improve, many times you win them over. This happens again and again.

Coaching

- As with the previous answer, this one is shows your generally good and professional attitude about your customers and your work.

- It would be a much better answer if you backed up your points by giving a specific example to prove what you are saying.

- The interviewer asked you to pick a situation—you needed to do that to do really well on your answer. By not bringing it down to a specific situation, your interviewer may perceive you as not having very good listening skills. I know you, so I know this isn't true. Next time, just pay a little closer attention and answer every part of questions you are asked.

Tell me about a time you had to persuade someone to do things the way you thought they should be done.

I had to convince executives that it was very important to develop a strategy focused on calling on bank customers. I persuaded them that it was critical to focus on the customers with the greatest revenue potential and to know which customer segment is the most profitable. Maybe we needed to focus on a different market segment if the customers did not meet the increased profitability goals.

Coaching

- Biggest question here: What was the outcome? Did you convince the executives? How did this benefit the bank?

- Always use positive language, not "I had to convince...."

- Provide more details in your answer (the way you provided them for the executives when you made your case to them). You will always be more credible as a candidate if you can site the numbers and details. This is particularly critical if you are in a profession using quantitative information and details, such as finance, engineering, accounting, or many areas of law.

- Ending your answer with a sentence starting, "Maybe we needed to focus..." would probably cause many interviewers to perceive you as hesitant and unsure of yourself. Try something that is more certain, such as, "After changing the sales strategy, the bank increased profitability by 10 percent the next year."

Chapter 12

Send a Thank-You Note, Follow Up, Get the Offer, and Negotiate

Imagine that you've just finished your final gymnastics routine at the 2008 Olympics. You've practiced for years and have spent a significant portion of your life on the bars or in floor exercises. You know you have worked hard with your coach, and you just gave a very good performance. Now you are waiting for your final score from the judges. Will you get the gold or the silver or the bronze medal?

Like the gymnast, you just finished your interview, and you liked the interviewers you met. This is your own version of the Olympics, because you know you really want this position.

The interviewers asked almost all of the competency-based interview questions you expected. Because you'd worked through the process of identifying the competencies and did a good job of anticipating questions, you were able to give thoughtful answers to prove how strong you are in each key competency area. And you know that you did well in the interview. Now you are waiting to find out whether you will get the offer.

You know you did a good job during the interview. You're ready to relax. But it is just a little too early. Don't celebrate yet. You aren't finished with the process. You haven't heard from the employer yet. What's left? First, you need to try to be as objective as possible and assess the interview. Ask yourself these questions:

- What did I do well?

- What could I have done during the interview to be perceived as a stronger candidate?

I believe that debriefing the interview is extremely important. Talk to your personal consultant or coach, go through the questions and answers, and look for opportunities to fine-tune your answers to make them more specific, concise, logical, or positive.

Ask yourself if there is anything you can think of that you did, verbally or nonverbally, that may have sent a negative message to the interviewers. You may be good, but you can always be better. I tell students in communications classes that I'd probably give Dr. Martin Luther King, Jr. a 98 or 99 on his "I Have a Dream" speech, which is generally considered one of the best speeches of the 20th century. Your interviewing skills, like your writing and presentation skills, can always improve to the next level.

So what else is important at this point? You need to send a good, competency-based thank-you note to the interviewers, and plan to follow up at the right time. When you get an offer, you may decide to negotiate with the employer. If you don't get an offer, you may choose to follow up to show the interviewer your interest in being considered for other opportunities in the future.

Send a Thank-You Note

During the interview, you remembered to ask for business cards from each interviewer you met. If they didn't have business cards with them, you made sure to include their names in your notes, which you made immediately after the interviews. You also jotted down some of the specific details that you remembered from each interview, so you would be able to write personal, nongeneric thank-you notes. And you made a list of the questions you were asked during the interview.

Thank-you notes are still important in today's world. They can make a positive difference in the interviewer's perception of you as a candidate. But they can also be negative. I've seen candidates eliminated by interviewers because they sent thank-you notes with poor grammar and smiley faces, or with the name of the interviewer or organization spelled incorrectly.

Remember that you want your thank-you notes to be perceived as polished and professional as you are. So proof your notes and put them through spell-check. Use:

- Capital letters at the beginning of sentences and in the places your teachers taught you.

- Complete sentences.

- Good punctuation, grammar, and spelling.

Avoid using smiley faces, Internet lingo such as lol, and emoticons such as :) in your thank-you notes.

In today's business environment, most candidates should to plan send their thank-you notes within 24 hours using e-mail. Think about the perception you want the interviewer to have of you. Using e-mail shows that you are current with technology and not outdated.

The only exception I can think of to this recommendation is with nonprofit organizations, where many professionals are still expected to write personal handwritten notes to donors and volunteers. According to Delphia York Duckens, Senior Vice President, Fund Development, Girl Scouts USA, even nonprofits are beginning to change. She told me, "We're starting to see e-mail used more for thank-you notes and other communication." So if you are trying to make a decision about whether to send your thank-you note to a nonprofit using e-mail or snail mail, consider how technologically advanced the nonprofit seems to be.

Send the thank-you note between the hours of 6 a.m. and midnight, when most people are awake. Remember, your e-mail will show the time it was sent. The only exception to the timing would be if your interview is for a position at night, on the "graveyard shift." Wait at least three hours after your interview to send the thank-you notes, so that the interviewers won't perceive you as desperate.

Steps to Writing a Good, Competency-Based Thank-You Note

Before you start writing the thank-you note, ask yourself these questions:

- What competencies did I learn the organization needs for the position I interviewed for?
- Was there a competency the interviewers mentioned that I didn't talk about in the interview? Or that I didn't give enough detail about my strengths?
- What did each interviewer discuss that I was impressed with?
- Was there something I left out that was important or that I could have explained better?
- What did I learn about the organization, the corporate culture, and the management style that will help me explain more effectively why I am a good match for the position?

When you write the thank-you note:

- Address each thank-you note to a specific interviewer, even if you had a group or panel interview. Individual, tailored thank-you notes are always more appreciated.
- First, tell the interviewer thank you—that you appreciate her time or the opportunity to have an interview. Tell her that you enjoyed meeting her and learning more about the position.

- Second, tell her something about how, after talking with her, you are even more interested in the position and are convinced that you would be successful in the position. Identify how your competencies match her needs (use competency synonyms to be a little more subtle but still get your point across) and will benefit her department or organization. Relate your comments to something that was said in the interview (for example, "I was particularly impressed when you talked to me about…).

- Third, tell her you are looking forward to hearing from her in the near future and would be happy to answer any questions or provide any additional information that she might need.

- Make sure you remember to put the interviewer's name at the top of the e-mail and your name at the bottom. If you want to start the e-mail with the words *Dear [interviewer name]*, make sure to close with a salutation (*Sincerely,*) before your name.

Always do a final edit to make sure the e-mail is a good reflection of your own professionalism.

Follow Up

At the end of the interview, most good interviewers should have told you:

- What the next steps were.

- What period of time they thought they'd need before getting back to you.

If they didn't give you this information, you should have directly asked for it at the end of the interview by saying, "I'm very interested in this opportunity. What's the next step?" Also ask them, "When is a good time for me to follow up with you?"

Many interviewers and human resources professionals are too optimistic about the timing and may, with good intentions, tell you they'll get back to you in a certain period of time—such as one or two weeks. When you work in an organization, the priorities keep changing, and sometimes there are good business reasons that the process takes longer than expected. During my years as a human resources professional, I learned to overestimate the time we'd need to give the candidate an answer to keep from disappointing him. Remember that the interviewers always have other important projects, assignments, and even a crisis or two to deal with. Manage your own expectations and give them the benefit of the doubt.

> *Learn to double the amount of time the interviewer tells you it will take to get back to you after an interview. Be pleasantly surprised if she is able to respond to you sooner.*

If the interviewer told you to follow up in two or three weeks, do it. Don't be a pest, but do be persistent and professional. Use your judgment, but please be respectful of the interviewer's time. Don't even think about calling daily unless you are interviewing for a position as a stalker. In most situations, following up every week or two is appropriate. If you are told the position has been put on hold, ask the interviewer when you should follow up to touch base with him.

If you receive an offer, make sure you call or e-mail the interviewers at other organizations you've interviewed with. Tell them that you've received an offer. If you are interested in their opportunity, let them know that you are still interested and it is your first choice (or one of your top choices).

Negotiate

Congratulations! You've just received a good job offer, and even though you are excited, you know it could be better. What should you do now?

- Thank the interviewer or human resources professional, and let him know that you really appreciate the offer.

- Ask for the offer in writing. Let the employer decide how to send it to you. In most cases today, they will probably e-mail the offer and explain how to look up information about benefits on the organization's Website.

- Tell the interviewer that you want to review all the information and that you are sure you are going to have some questions. Ask if it would work for him if you called him in two or three days with your answer (or questions).

- Talk to your network to help you do some intelligence work. Our president in the United States may have the CIA, but most of us can find out all sorts of information that could help us negotiate more effectively from the people we know—or the people they know. Remember the theory behind six degrees of separation: that we can get to anyone we want (or find anything we need) if we ask our contact's contact's contact's contact's contact.

- Try to find out information about the salary range for the position in your geographic area, whether the organization will negotiate, what's normal for vacation, and what special deals (signing bonuses, car allowances, bonuses, benefits, memberships, and so forth) the organization may have offered other people in similar jobs or at a similar level.

- Do your homework and know what is likely to be negotiable and what is not. I'm just going to give you a few guidelines here to help you with this process. Salary and vacation are certainly negotiable in many organizations, particularly once you've had a few years of work experience. Qualified benefit plans, including 401(k)s or other retirement plans, are set up organization-wide and are heavily regulated. Don't waste your bargaining chip trying to get an organization to make an exception for you on a plan that has legal restrictions. If you are working with a recruiter, he or she may know some of this information—or be willing to help you find out.

- Realize that negotiating well requires good information and good judgment. Each situation is different, and it is difficult to identify a set of rules that work in all situations. You probably would benefit by talking about the offer to someone with inside information or a good knowledge of the market in your field.

- If you decide to negotiate, remember that your goal is win-win. You want the people you'll be working with to *want* to work with you after you've finished negotiating and accepted the position. Identify your top three to five priorities that you want to negotiate, and go through them during your first conversation. It is not fair to settle things one at a time and then come back to negotiate the next priority. You may get what you want in the short-term but lose the long-term trust you need to build effective working relationships and do the job. So treat the person representing the organization in the negotiation, whether your future manager or human resources professional, with respect.

- Always emphasize the positives at the beginning of any negotiation, and let the other person know how excited you are about the opportunity. Tell the person representing the organization how impressed you are with the people there, and list everything good about the opportunity that you can think of. Then, explain again why you are such a good match or fit for the position. After that, say something like, "I have to admit I was a little disappointed with the [salary, vacation, and so on], and I'm wondering if there's room to negotiate." Then pause and see what the person says.

- Remember the old saying, "If you don't ask, you won't get." You'll rarely have regrets if you negotiate with respect and professionalism, and you just may get what you want—and feel even better about accepting the job opportunity.

By the way, the judges just came back. Don't tell anyone, but you *did* win the gold.

Key Points for Chapter 12	
Don't be a pest, but do be persistent and professional. *If you don't ask, you won't get.*	
Key Questions	**Answers**
When you finish the interview, can you relax?	Not yet. You need to debrief the interview, send a competency-based thank-you note, and follow up at appropriate times.
What questions do you need to ask yourself after the interview?	What did I do well during the interview?
	What could I have done to be perceived as a stronger candidate by the interviewer?
What information do you need before writing your thank-you notes?	Make sure you have the correct names and titles for each interviewer and the right e-mail addresses.
How should you send your thank-you note to the interviewer?	Use e-mail unless you have a very good reason to use snail mail. Send the thank-you note by e-mail within the first 24 hours after you leave the interview, but not within the first three hours. Remember to avoid sending any e-mail to an employer between midnight and 6 a.m., unless you are interviewing for a position working for the "graveyard shift."
What else should you remember about the thank-you note?	• Don't be too informal in your e-mail thank-you note. Capitalize where appropriate, check spelling/punctuation/grammar, and avoid Internet lingo and emoticons. • Write individualized notes to each interviewer. • Edit the note and put it through a spell-check.

Key Questions	Answers
How do you write a competency-based thank-you note?	Look for an opportunity to include something in the thank-you note about how your experience addresses the competencies the employer needs to be successful. Back up your point about the relevant experience by giving a specific example.
When should you follow up after the interview?	It depends. Hopefully, at the end of the interview, the interviewer told you when you could expect to hear something. *Double the timeframe the interviewer gave you.* If the interviewer told you when to follow up, call when you were told to call.
What should you do immediately when you get an offer?	<ul><li>Thank the person giving you the offer.</li><li>Ask for the offer in writing.</li><li>Tell the interviewer you're sure that you're going to have some questions, and you'll get back to her once you've reviewed the offer and benefits.</li></ul>
Why should you try to negotiate with the employer?	Many employers will offer you only the basics because they expect you to negotiate. If you don't ask for the extra vacation, salary, sign-on bonus, or better relocation package, you won't get it. If you don't try, you may regret it. If you do negotiate, you just may come out ahead!

Key Questions	Answers
What is important to do to prepare for negotiating with an employer?	• Do some intelligence work—learn about typical salaries for the position in your geographic area, whether the organization has a history of negotiating, what's normal for vacation, and other benefits and perks. • Know what is usually negotiable (salary and vacations, for example) and what is never negotiable (401k and other retirement vehicles). • Decide the most important item to negotiate, and then two to three other things to focus on during your negotiation with the employer.
What outcome do you want when you negotiate your offer?	Win-win. You want to get the most you can while ensuring the key people at the employer still want to work with you.

Chapter 13

Actively Manage Your Career in Competency-Based Organizations

Look at a day when you are supremely satisfied at the end. It's not a day when you lounge around doing nothing; it's when you've had everything to do, and you've done it.
—Margaret Thatcher

Congratulations! You've learned what it takes to win in a competency-based interview, and you are getting ready to start that great job you really wanted. You're excited about the opportunity and you want to do well.

What do you need to know to actively manage your career in a new, competency-based organization? Or to capitalize on your promotion to a new position in a different part of your own organization?

When you were in school, you learned that the best students made an effort to understand their assignments and do what the teachers asked. Robert Fulghum makes the case that we probably learned this type of behavior when we were very young in his book , *All I Really Need to Know I Learned in Kindergarten*. In your new position, you need to be a good student again. It is important to understand the system and learn how to work within it if you want to be successful.

You've already taken the first few steps toward managing your career in a competency-based organization. You've identified the competencies you need to be successful in the position, and you've thought about how your accomplishments help prove you are competent in the most critical areas. In addition, you've learned how to talk about your accomplishments to be able to answer competency-based behavioral questions.

As you continue your career, you need to be aware of how important it is to build, track, and master the *right* competencies. To help ensure you are perceived as the star that I know you are, I have seven suggestions for what you can do to actively manage your career the competency-based way:

1. Learn to write competency-based accomplishment statements to use in employee development plans, self-appraisals, and other situations.

2. Set up and use a system to track your competencies.

3. Develop your critical competencies to a higher level.

4. Identify and overcome your competency gaps, if you need to.

5. Work towards developing competencies you'll need for future positions.

6. Promote your career by making sure your managers know your competencies.

7. Give your manager a current list of your accomplishments in each key competency area before your performance appraisal.

Let's look at each of these recommendations in more detail.

Learn to Write Competency-Based Accomplishment Statements to Use in Employee Development Plans, Self-Appraisals, and Other Situations

Think about your answers to competency-based interview questions. As you prepared for the interview, you put together a list of your accomplishments in each relevant competency area.

You've already done the thinking about your examples. Now you just have to turn them into true accomplishment statements— in other words, write them down!

Here are a few other tips about how to write good competency-based accomplishment statements:

- Focus on your accomplishments proving your competencies.

- Say as much as you can in as few words as you can. Don't use complete sentences or extra words that don't add to the content, such as *a, an, the, various,* and *numerous*.

- Always start with an action verb.

- Make sure you've thought through the situation/task/ problem, action, and results parts of every accomplishment. Decide whether the result, the action, or the process is going to matter the most to the employer and make that the first part of your accomplishment statement.

- Try to give numbers, statistics, or financial figures to help the reader understand the scope of the assignment or project. Be specific and give enough details to be credible.

- Assume the readers are intelligent but may not know the details about your immediate business or professional area.

- Make your accomplishment statements as strong as you can without lying. Remember: We talked about *spinning* your answer in as positive a way as possible while still being honest in Chapters 4 and 5.

- Try to include high-profile examples that your senior executives might know about, whenever possible.

A few examples of good competency-based accomplishment statements:

- Worked as key member of focus group looking at best practices for data management; helped create business case for buying more disk space.

- Recognized by vice president for successfully leading project team reducing utility processing from three hours to 10 minutes per day and increasing accuracy 30 percent; improved customer relationships with six major clients.

Set Up and Use a System to Track Your Competencies

It is important to spend some time thinking about setting up a system to track your accomplishments and the competencies that are demonstrated in each accomplishment. Very few, if any, organizations have developed this kind of system for their employees, so you probably need to think about setting up a system that will work for you. Whether you use a Word table, an Excel spreadsheet, an Access database, software programs for your PDA or BlackBerry, or an old-fashioned paper filing system, you should include accomplishments related to:

- The competencies identified for your current position.

- The competencies you would need for positions you would like to be considered for in the future.

Develop Your Critical Competencies to a Higher Level

Once you know the critical competencies for your current position, you need to identify the accomplishments that prove your own competence in each area. Look for opportunities to gain experience showing that your work is at an even higher, more sophisticated level of competency. Ask your manager to be considered for certain assignments. Find a mentor or a coach to help you develop. Take classes offered by your organization or at colleges and universities or in the community. Consider doing volunteer work or teaching classes at a university or college to build your competencies.

Identify and Overcome Your Competency Gaps, if You Need To

In some cases, your weakest competency areas can offer you the biggest opportunities for growth. What are the competencies that you cannot prove because you do not have any direct experience in that area to draw from? These are your competency gaps, and you may make the decision that they need to be developed, bridged, and overcome.

In many cases, though, people decide that they can compensate for their gaps by using other competencies. Perception matters. The key question in this case is this: Does your manager perceive the gap as a weakness that needs to be overcome? If he does, work on it!

When a good employee transfers into another functional area, it is reasonable to expect some competency gaps. Think about an engineer transferring into finance or sales. Or a human resources manager who becomes a line manager in manufacturing. In these cases, the new manager and other key people typically put together an extensive on-the-job and classroom training schedule, and actively coach the transferred employee. Everyone benefits when the transfer is recognized as successful and the transferred employee has overcome his competency gaps.

Work Towards Developing Competencies You'll Need for Future Positions

What kind of position do you want for your next assignment, or in five or 10 years? In addition to the competencies you need for your current position, you need to start doing some work *now* that will help you prove you have the competencies you need for higher level positions *later*. If you consciously do this, when you are being considered for your next promotion, it should be clear to the critical decision-makers that you have been working at that higher level for some time. You've proved your competence in the key areas required to do a good job.

Promote Your Career by Making Sure Your Managers Know Your Competencies

Have you ever complained that you didn't get an assignment or position because the manager making the decision didn't realize that you had experience in a certain area? Don't let that happen to you another time. Try to make sure that your managers know about your competencies and accomplishments that are *not* being used in your current position, but that could be used in the future.

For example, if you know your company is looking at an acquisition in Argentina and you lived there for three years before college, make sure the *right* managers know that you have those *interpersonal understanding* or *multicultural sensitivity* competencies, and that you can prove them. Even if you mentioned it to your manager two years ago in your interview, remind her that you are bicultural and bilingual and would love to have the opportunity to work on the acquisition.

When you have an accomplishment related to one of the critical competencies for your position, make sure your manager knows. Simply call your manager over to your office to tell her how excited you are because a particular project is going well, and make sure you give her any results that you know. If you are working virtual, make sure you include the news about your accomplishment in telephone sessions with your manager.

Give Your Manager a Current List of Your Accomplishments in Each Key Competency Area Before Your Performance Appraisal

Because you've been tracking your accomplishments by competency area for several months or a year, you should be ready to provide this information to your manager whenever it may help him. But for your own career, one of the best times to make sure your manager has an updated list of easy to understand, well written, thorough, and concise accomplishments is three or four weeks before your performance appraisal. List each accomplishment under the most relevant competency. You may also want to identify the other competencies shown by the accomplishment for your manager.

Conclusion

If you consider competencies when you actively manage your career, and you follow the tips in this chapter, you will be ahead of most of the people that you currently consider your competition in the organization. I'm not surprised. I always thought you were a star.

Key Points for Chapter 13	
The best job goes to the person who can get it done without passing the buck or coming back with excuses. —Napoleon Hill	
Key Questions	**Answers**
What can you do to manage your career the competency-based way?	• Learn to write competency-based accomplishment statements to use in employee development plans, self-appraisals, and other situations.

Key Questions	Answers
What can you do to manage your career the competency-based way? (*Continued*)	<ul><li>Set up and use a system to track your competencies.</li><li>Develop your most critical competencies to a hight level.</li><li>Identify and overcome your competency gaps.</li><li>Work towards developing competencies you will need for future positions.</li><li>Promote your career and accomplishments to your managers.</li><li>Give your manager a list of your accomplishments in each competency area immediately before your performance appraisal.</li></ul>
What should you keep in mind when you write competency-based accomplishment statements?	<ul><li>Focus on your accomplishments proving competencies.</li><li>Say as much as you can in as few words as you can.</li><li>Don't use complete sentences or extra words that don't add to the content.</li><li>Always start with an action verb.</li><li>Make sure you have thought about the situation/task/problem, action, and results portion of each of your accomplishments.</li><li>Decide whether the result, the action, or the process is going to matter the most to the employer and make that the first part of your accomplishment statement.</li><li>Make your statements as strong as you can without lying. *Spin* your answer.</li></ul>

Key Questions	Answers
	• Try to give numbers, statistics, or financial figures to help the reader understand the project/assignment scope. Be specific and give enough details to be credible. • Assume the readers are intelligent but may not know the details about your immediate business or professional area. • Try to include high-profile examples that your senior executives might know about, whenever possible.
What type of system should you set up to track your competencies?	If your employer doesn't have a system, figure out what will work the best for you. You can use a Word table, Excel spreadsheet, database, PDA software, or old-fashioned filing system.
What do you need to track?	Accomplishments and the competencies they show.
What do you need to remember when you have input into your training and development or future assignments?	Use these opportunities to develop your competencies to a higher level for your current position and future job possibilities. You can also use this as a way to overcome any competency gaps you need to overcome.
What else is important to do in a competency-based organization	• Communicate with your managers about your accomplishments in key competency areas. • Don't be too modest. • Use the language of competencies. • Give your manager a list of your accomplishments sorted by competency area three to four weeks before your performance appraisal.

Chapter 14

Use Competency-Based Resumes to Get Your Next Interview

Man's mind, once stretched by a new idea, never regains its original dimensions.
—Oliver Wendell Holmes

When I read Oliver Wendell Holmes's quote about how a new idea stretches a person's mind so it can never be the way it was before, I thought about my new idea: competency-based resumes. It's true that my mind has never been the same, and I'd really like to think it is better. So, in this case, with all my personal respect to Mr. Holmes, please substitute the words *A person's mind* for *Man's mind* in the quote.

Giving employees some background so they can learn to thrive in a competency-based organization is another new idea. You've spent most of this book learning how you can be more successful in a competency-based interview to help you get the job you really want.

In Chapter 13, you learned how to write competency-based accomplishment statements to help you advocate for yourself when you are writing your self-evaluations and employee development plans. You also started thinking about how to track and develop your competencies, and how to communicate more effectively with your managers about your competencies. You're in that great job now, you're doing well, and you've proven how competent you are over a period of time.

But don't let yourself get too comfortable. It's time to stretch yourself by starting to think about your *next* opportunity, and you need to be ready. It's time to write your *first* competency-based resume, or to revise the competency-based resume you used to win your last position.

Why You Should Write a Competency-Based Resume

Competency-based resumes are much more effective than more traditional resumes. They give you an edge with employers because they are more focused and target the competencies the employers are looking for in today's labor market. Competency-based resumes consider the employer's needs *first*, then help *prove* you match what the employer is looking for. A well written, competency-based resume includes crisp, targeted accomplishment statements and a summary section aimed at the competencies the employer needs to be successful now and in the future.

Why should you use a competency-based resume? It will sell your experience more effectively to employers and increase your chance of getting the interview. Even in non competency-based organizations, a competency-based resume will give you an edge because it is written to target the real needs of the employer.

Steps to Writing a Competency-Based Resume

The approach to writing competency-based resumes is different from the way you may have written your resume in the past. To write a good competency-based resume, you need to follow these steps:

1. Identify competencies for the position.

2. Think about what you have done that demonstrates expertise or experience with each of the competencies.

3. Develop accomplishment statements for as many of the competencies as you can.

4. Write the summary section so it emphasizes your experience and strengths related to the key competencies for the position.

5. Determine which competency-based resume format—chronological, functional, direct competency, or combination—best fits your needs, and prepare your first draft of the resume.

6. Remember to include sections on your education and any other specific information relevant to potential employers.

7. Add additional competency-related accomplishment statements and, if you still have space, other accomplishment statements.

8. Prioritize competency-related phrases in your summary section and competency-based accomplishments within the appropriate sections of the resume.

9. Review and polish your resume. Ask other professionals for input.

10. Finalize your resume. Develop an electronic version of the resume with a keyword summary section.

Writing a good, competency-based resume should make sense to you. You've already read Chapter 2 and gone through the process of identifying competencies for your last position. Now you need to repeat the process and identify the competencies for the new position you are interested in.

You've also learned how to write effective competency-based accomplishment statements and have kept track of your accomplishments in a good table, spreadsheet, database, or filing system. Look at Chapter 13 if you want to review these career management tips, and pull out your list of accomplishments before beginning to write your resume.

Example of a Competency-Based Resume

Let's look at one example of a competency-based resume. This particular resume is a competency-based functional resume for the same financial sales professional whose answers to competency-based interview questions are included in Chapter 10. We chose to use this format because we wanted to emphasize her accomplishments in certain key categories that were important to the organization she was interested in working for.

Donna Johnson's resume, shown on pages 204–207, is one example of a good competency-based resume. Please know that I helped my client write this resume, but a few changes have been made to protect her privacy. I've changed her name, contact information, and the name of an employer or two.

Once Donna identified the position she was interested in, we were able to determine the key competencies and write targeted competency-based accomplishment statements. Then we worked on the summary section.

Please know that what makes a resume competency-based is the content, not the format. Each accomplishment statement is competency-based. The summary also addresses the competencies.

> *What makes a resume competency-based is the content.*

There's more than one format for competency-based resumes. In addition to competency-based fuctional resumes, you can choose to write competency-based chronological resumes that *look* more traditional and focus on your work history with accomplishments listed under each job. Direct competency resumes list your accomplishments by competency and are good to use when you want to provide your manager with a list of your accomplishments before your performance appraisal.

Summary or Profile

This section is one of the most important parts of any resume because, if it is well written, it sells your background to the employer. *It has replaced the objective* on the resume because it is so much more effective at communicating the most important reasons the employer should consider you for the position.

One approach to writing a good summary section is to start with what you call yourself professionally or the title listed for the position you are interested in. Then write about your expertise, your job-related strengths, and your strengths in the relevant competency areas. Some career experts like to do a bulleted list of your strengths; others don't.

Please be aware that career coaches have different styles of writing summary sections. To make sure that your resume opens the right doors for you, just be sure your summary is competency-based.

Technical Skills

You should plan to have a technical skills section if you work in IT or another technical area where your knowledge of software, hardware, or specific technical tools is required before a hiring manager will consider you for a position.

Education

Please make every effort to check this section of your resume to make sure it is accurate. Although I believe in putting the best possible spin you can on your background, you either have a college degree or you don't.

Every year, it seems that we hear about a new example of someone who is in trouble for claiming a degree that he doesn't quite have. For example, in 2002, the athletic director for Dartmouth College resigned after his employer found out that he had not completed the master's degree he had listed on his resume. Please know that your educational credentials can be easily checked by the employer.

As a general rule, if your degree is more than 10 years old, leave the graduation date off your resume.

Donna B. Johnson

3202 Jasmine
Denver, CO 80205

303-555-5249
djohnson2@sbcglobal.net

SUMMARY

Finance professional with strong interest in financial analysis and sales. Proven track record of developing financial models to streamline processes. Recognized for consistent ranking as top producer, understanding complex financial information and communicating financial data to clients to encourage investment. Strengths include results orientation, analytical and teaching/training skills, resourcefulness and initiative.

Licenses: Series 7, 63, 65 and 24 and Group 1.

ACCOMPLISHMENTS

Financial Analysis

- Recognized for developing first proprietary sell-to-cover model at company to calculate number of stock options to sell at set market price; increased customer satisfaction 15% and created opportunity for additional commissions.

- Developed first Excel spreadsheet at company to calculate taxes for exercising stock options for United Kingdom residents; provided competitive advantage to obtain 100% of IBM stock option business in United Kingdom; provided additional $90,000 per year in gross commission.

- Audited online system for exercising stock options at firm; analyzed data and recommended changes to improve visual presentation and quality of customer directions; increased online order submission 5%.

- Prepared competitive analysis of financial statements for five major oil companies while working as summer intern at Amoco.

Financial Sales/Marketing

- Ranked in top four of 40 retirement specialists nationally at Fidelity for 12 consecutive months, 2001-2002.

- Identified opportunity to increase assets by allowing customers to maintain their investments positions; persuaded three senior managers to support change in business practice; increased retained assets by 20%.

- Increased long term care insurance sales by 10%; designed and delivered long term care sales seminar for 15 retail brokers.

- Produced $189k in first year commissions as Financial Advisor at American Express; ranked in top 25% of peer group.

- Recognized by manager for increasing small loan revenues 25%; created solicitation campaign for loans between $500-$1,000.

- Developed risk management program to collect delinquent accounts; reduced 30 day delinquency 30%.

Financial Training/Planning

- Trained 15 financial consultants on how to educate clients about annuities, long term care insurance and health insurance; increased sales 30%.

- Delivered training program on mortgage disclosure documentation, loan documentation and loan processing using proprietary system to 40 new employees.

- Developed training for 27 financial advisors at American Express on presenting client seminars for retirement, planning, college planning and estate planning.

- Created financial plans for 150 individuals and 30 small businesses as American Express Financial Advisor 1998-2000.

Donna B. Johnson

Page 2

WORK HISTORY

NATIONAL FINANCIAL, Denver, CO
Stock Options Department Supervisor, 2003-2005
Financial Consultant, 2002-2003

2002-2005

FIDELITY INVESTMENTS, Denver, CO
Senior Retirement Specialist

2000-2002

AMERICAN EXPRESS FINANCIAL ADVISORS, Dallas, TX
Financial Advisor, 1998-2000

1998-2000

BENEFICIAL INC., Denver, CO
Branch Manager, 1996-1998
Assistant Branch Manager, 1995-1996
Branch Service Manager, 1994-1995

1994-1998

EDUCATION

Bachelor of Science, Marketing and International Business
University of Colorado, Boulder, CO

Other Competency-Based Resume Tips

- Prioritize your accomplishments on the resume within each section to emphasize the experience and competencies that matter the most to the employer.

- Expect to use two pages on your resume unless you have less than 10 years of work experience. Then you should plan on having a one-page resume.

- Always have an e-mail address that sounds professional and benign as part of your contact information. Consider setting up a new e-mail address just for your job search.

- Use your cell phone number on the resume. Don't waste space identifying that a phone number is a phone number or an e-mail is an e-mail.

- If you include an "Other Information" or "Community Activities" section, only include information proving you'd be effective at a specific job. Don't include anything controversial such as religion or politics unless you are interested in a position with a church, mosque or temple, an organization such as Catholic Charities, the Republican or Democratic parties, or an elected official.

- If you have some special issues, such as not working for an extended period of time, consider talking with a professional about the best way to handle your situation on the resume. You might want to use a competency-based functional resume, to help the reader focus more on your accomplishments than on your work history. If you have been in one position for more than five years, you might choose to write a combination-style resume, which would show your accomplishments in your most recent job broken into a few important categories or competencies. Each situation is different, and a savvy professional can help you figure out the best way to position your resume to show your competencies and strengths the most effectively.

- Plan to rewrite or revise your resume and cover letter for every new job opportunity. Once you have developed your first competency-based resume, though, you should have most of the information you'll need to target future opportunities.

If you want more help with writing competency-based resumes, read the book *Competency-Based Resumes: How to Bring Your Resume to the Top of the Pile* (Career Press, November 2004) for more examples and details about how to write extremely good resumes targeting the competencies the employers need. (If you like *Competency-Based Interviews*, I'm confident that you'll also enjoy *Competency-Based Resumes*.)

Key Points for Chapter 14	
Focusing on the competencies the employer is looking for is a very powerful way to approach one's next job. —*Ward Klein, President and Chief Operating Officer, Energizer*	
Key Questions	**Answers**
Why should you write a competency-based resume?	Competency-based resumes: • Are more effective. • Are more focused and targeted to meet the employer's needs. • Sell your experience that matters .
What are the steps to writing a competency-based resume?	1. Identify competencies. 2. Think about what you have done that demonstrates experience with each key competency. 3. Develop accomplishment statements for as many of the competencies as you can. 4. Write the summary section to emphasize your experience and strengths related to the key competencies for the position. 5. Determine which competency-based resume format (chrono- logical, functional, direct competency, or combination) best fits your needs, and prepare your first draft of the resume.

Key Questions	Answers
What are the steps to writing a competency-based resume? (*Contintued*)	6. Remember to include sections on your education and any other specific information which might be relevant to potential employers. 7. Add additional competency-related accomplishment statements, and, if you still have extra space, other accomplishment statements. 8. Prioritize the competency-related phrases in your summary section and your competency-based accomplishments within appropriate sections. 9. Review and polish your resume. Ask others for their input. 10. Finalize your resume. Develop an electronic version of the resume with a keyword summary section.
What makes a resume competency-based?	The content, not the format.
What are the different formats you could use for a competency-based resume?	• Competency-based chronological • Competency-based functional • Direct competency • Combination
What is important to remember about the "Summary" section of your resume?	• It is extremely important because if it is well-written, it will sell your background to the employer. • Start with a professional title, then write about your expertise, job-related strengths, and your strengths in the relevant competency areas.
When should you include a "Technical Skills" section in your resume?	If you work in IT or another area where your knowledge of hardware, software, or technical tools is required before the employer will consider you for a position.

Key Questions	Answers
What is important to remember for the "Education" section of your resume?	• Don't ever claim a degree or educational credential you don't have. • If your degree is more than 10 years old, don't include your graduation date.
What other tips should you know before writing a competency-based resume?	• Prioritize your accomplishments within each section to emphasize experience and competencies that matter the most to the employer. • Expect to use two pages on your resume unless you have less than 10 years of work experience. • Say as much as you can in as few words as you can. • Always use an e-mail address that sounds professional as part of your contact information. • Use your cell phone number on the resume. • Don't waste space identifying that a phone number is a phone number or an e-mail is an e-mail. • If you include an "Other Information" or "Community Activities" section, only include information proving you'd be effective at a specific job. Don't include anything controversial such as religion or politics, as a general rule. • If you have some special issues, consider talking with a professional about the best way to handle them on the resume. • Plan to rewrite or revise your resume for every new job opportunity.
If you want to learn more about competency-based resumes, what should you do?	Read *Competency-Based Resumes: How to Bring Your Resume to the Top of the Pile* (Career Press, 2004).

Chapter 15

Think Long-Term and Make Change Work for You

The real voyage of discovery consists not in seeking new landscapes, but in having new eyes.
—Marcel Proust

When I first read Proust's quote, I thought about the changes competencies have brought to the landscape for people who want to work at the best, most sophisticated employers. In this book, you've learned some important ways to make the competency-based systems at today's best organizations work for you.

Competencies have been used in the business world for more than 20 years now, but today's competency-based systems are more sophisticated than they used to be. They are continuing to grow and evolve. You don't have to seek a new landscape—the landscape has changed. The landscape has changed everywhere, and your job is to make sure that you notice the changes.

Because some employees and candidates resist change, they may never see that the system has changed around them. Many of us can remember secretaries who didn't think they had to learn about computers or word processing. Technology changed the landscape. If they didn't change their own view and learn to work with computers, those secretaries became obsolete.

> *If you don't recognize change and adapt, you'll become obsolete.*

What can we expect for the future? How will the landscape change? How will our perception of those changes affect our success?

In the short term, you can expect more and more organizations to continue to work with competencies. It just makes sense.

If your organization isn't working with competencies yet, it may be in the future. Thinking about what is most important to your employer first will help you be more successful even in a non competency-based organization.

Many of the most sophisticated employers have worked closely with consultants to develop effective competency-based human resources systems that are working well for them. Managers at these organizations usually decided to use competency-based systems because they saw it as a way to help them improve the overall performance of their employees.

Those organizations with good competency-based systems are in a strong position to build the key characteristics that it will take to be even more successful in the future. Their managers recruit, interview, and hire employees who are strong in the competencies they need. They evaluate their employees based on goals and competencies, and coach or train their employees to develop the competencies the organization needs to ensure success.

The best organizations have invested considerable time and money into these competency-based systems. But are they working as well as they could? Based on my consulting, the answer is no.

Employers need to collaborate with their employees to make their competency-based systems work more effectively. There are six major reasons it makes sense for employers to partner with employees and make more of an effort to explain their own competency-based system to their employees[1]:

1. *To improve the competency levels of their employees faster.* If each employee understands the competency-based system and takes responsibility for managing the relevant competencies (in addition to training or coaching provided by the organization), the overall competency levels within the organization will improve much faster.

2. *To provide managers with better information about the competencies of their employees.* If employees advocate for themselves more effectively by providing better-written, clearer, competency-based information about their accomplishments, or if they are able to give good explanations during competency-based interviews, it will give managers the information they need to make better decisions about assignments and opportunities.

3. *To enable companies to sell their services more effectively to competency-based customers.* For companies providing consulting, engineering, project management, or architectural work to competency-based organizations, it just makes sense for the proposed project team to develop competency-based resumes to include in the proposal package targeting the competencies the decision-makers are measured against. When the competency-based customer asks to interview the project team, the interviewees will be more successful if they are prepared for competency-based interviews. (Please know that improving

the way you present your employees cannot overcome an extremely high bid for the contract. But it can make a difference in other cases.)

4.   *To empower employees and improve morale.* If employees understand what they can do to actively manage their careers in competency-based systems, they are much more likely to buy into the system and be committed to making it work.

5.   *To support diversity efforts.* By making more of an effort to train employees about competencies in their organizations, employers are demystifying what it takes to get ahead. On a practical level, they are helping to clarify the rules for everyone, without regard to race, sex, age, national origin, or disability status. More employees have a chance to be successful, and more types of employees *will* be successful.

6.   *To improve the quality of employee development and succession planning.* If managers have better access to good information about the competencies of the candidates for promotions, they can do a better job with succession planning. Learning to communicate more effectively about your competencies to managers simply helps the key decision-makers make better decisions about your future opportunities.

Because it makes business sense, expect to see the better employers offer their employees more training about what they can do to be successful in the organization's competency-based system. When I've worked with managers at companies such as American Express and BP to offer this type of program, there's been a strong level of interest from the employees. They recognize that the system has changed, and they want to know what they can do to be more successful on the new playing field.

At BP, the human resources department in Houston sponsored a pilot program called "How to Thrive in BP's Competency-Based System." My contact in human resources sent an e-mail to 200 people inviting them to a lunch-and-learn session a few months ago. Within an hour, 100 people had responded saying they were interested in attending.

At American Express, one of the IT directors sponsored an initial program teaching employees how to thrive in their own competency-based system. I trained them to be more aware of the relevant competencies and showed them examples of competency-based accomplishment statements. The next step, which has already been scheduled, focuses on teaching the same group how to write effective competency-based accomplishment statements for their employee development plans and employee questionnaires before mid-year and year-end performance reviews.

In addition to formally sponsored training programs, special interest groups within the larger companies sometimes bring in guest speakers. The Women's Network within JPMorganChase sponsored me to come in and speak to its members about how to be more successful working within its competency-based system.

When you see your own organization begin to offer these types of programs to give employees tools that they can use to thrive with competencies, make sure you are one of the first to take advantage of the opportunity.

Learn everything you can about the competencies for your current position and possible future positions. Think about what competencies are important for success now and in the future. Of course, while you're doing that, remember to continue to do your job.

Understanding how competencies can work for you and help you be more successful is critical to help you plan and navigate your career for the future. Being smart and using this information to help advocate for yourself within your organization can make a difference.

Learning about competencies can help you see your professional future with new eyes. Your eyes may still be brown or blue or green or hazel, but your vision will be clearer, and you can now come closer to seeing your goal for your career.

Appendix A:
List of Core
Competencies

I. Competencies Dealing With People

The Leading Others Cluster

☐ Establishing Focus: The ability to develop and communicate goals in support of the business mission.

- Acts to align own unit's goals with the strategic direction of the business.

- Ensures that people in the unit understand how their work relates to the business mission.

- Ensures that everyone understands and identifies with the unit's mission.

- Ensures that the unit develops goals and a plan to help fulfill the business mission.

☐ Providing Motivational Support: The ability to enhance others' commitment to their work.

- Recognizes and rewards people for their achievements.

- Acknowledges and thanks people for their contributions.

- Expresses pride in the group and encourages people to feel good about their accomplishments.

- Finds creative ways to make people's work rewarding.

- Signals own commitment to a process by being personally present and involved at key events.

- Identifies and promptly tackles morale problems.

- Gives talks or presentations that energize groups.

☐ Fostering Teamwork: As a team member, the ability and desire to work cooperatively with others on a team; as a team leader, the ability to demonstrate interest, skill, and success in getting groups to learn to work together.

Behavior for Team Members

- Listens and responds constructively to other team members' ideas.

- Offers support for others' ideas and proposals.

- Is open with other team members about his/her concerns.

- Expresses disagreement constructively.

- Reinforces team members for their contributions.

- Gives honest and constructive feedback to other team members.

- Provides assistance to others when they need it.

- Works for solutions that all team members can support.

- Shares his/her expertise with others.

- Seeks opportunities to work on teams as a means to develop experience and knowledge.

- Provides assistance, information, or support to others to build or maintain relationships with them.

Behavior for Team Leaders

- Provides opportunities for people to learn to work together as a team.

- Enlists the active participation of everyone.

- Promotes cooperation with other work units.

- Ensures that all team members are treated fairly.

- Recognizes and encourages the behaviors that contribute to teamwork.

☐ Empowering Others: The ability to convey confidence in the ability of employees to be successful, especially at challenging new tasks; delegating significant responsibility and authority; allowing employees freedom to decide how they will accomplish their goals and resolve issues.

- Gives people latitude to make decisions in their own sphere of work.

- Is able to let others make decisions and take charge.

- Encourages individuals and groups to set their own goals, consistent with business goals.

- Expresses confidence in the ability of others to be successful.

- Encourages groups to resolve problems on their own; avoids prescribing a solution.

☐ Managing Change: The ability to demonstrate support for innovation and for organizational changes needed to improve the organization's effectiveness; initiating, sponsoring, and implementing organizational change; helping others to successfully manage organizational change.

Employee Behaviors

- Personally develops a new method or approach.

- Proposes new approaches, methods, or technologies.

- Develops better, faster, or less expensive ways to do things.

Manager/Leader Behaviors

- Works cooperatively with others to produce innovative solutions.

- Takes the lead in setting new business directions, partnerships, policies, or procedures.

- Seizes opportunities to influence the future direction of an organizational unit or the overall business.

- Helps employees to develop a clear understanding of what they will need to do differently, as a result of changes in the organization.

- Implements or supports various change management activities.

- Establishes structures and processes to plan and manage the orderly implementation of change.

- Helps individuals and groups manage the anxiety associated with significant change.

- Facilitates groups or teams through the problem-solving and creative-thinking processes leading to the development and implementation of new approaches, systems, structures, and methods.

☐ Developing Others: The ability to delegate responsibility and to work with others and coach them to develop their capabilities.

- Provides helpful, behaviorally specific feedback to others.

- Shares information, advice, and suggestions to help others be more successful; provides effective coaching.

- Gives people assignments that will help develop their abilities.

- Regularly meets with employees to review their developmental progress.

- Recognizes and reinforces people's developmental efforts and improvements.

- Expresses confidence in the ability of others to be successful.

☐ Managing Performance: The ability to take responsibility for one's own, or one's employees' performance, by setting clear goals and expectations, tracking progress against the goals, ensuring feedback, and addressing performance problems and issues promptly.

Employee Behaviors

- With his manager, sets specific, measurable goals that are realistic but challenging, with dates for accomplishment.

- With his manager, clarifies expectations about what will be done and how.

- Enlists his manager's support in obtaining the information, resources, and training needed to accomplish his work effectively.

- Promptly notifies his manager about any problems that affect his ability to accomplish planned goals.

- Seeks performance feedback from his manager and from others with whom he interacts on the job.

- Prepares a personal development plan with specific goals and a timeline for their accomplishment.

- Takes significant action to develop skills needed for effectiveness in current or future job.

Manager/Leader Behaviors

- Ensures that employees have clear goals and responsibilities.

- Works with employees to set and communicate performance standards that are specific and measurable.

- Supports employees in their efforts to achieve job goals.

- Stays informed about employees' progress and performance through both formal and informal methods.

- Provides specific performance feedback, both positive and corrective, as soon as possible after an event.

- Deals firmly and promptly with performance problems; lets people know what is expected of them and when.

Communication and Influencing Cluster

☐ Attention to Communication: The ability to ensure that information is passed on to others who should be kept informed.

- Ensures that others involved in a project or effort are kept informed about developments and plans.

- Ensures that important information from his management is shared with his employees and others as appropriate.

- Shares ideas and information with others who might find them useful.

- Uses multiple channels or means to communicate important messages.

- Keeps his manager informed about progress and problems; avoids surprises.

- Ensures that regular, consistent communication takes place.

☐ Oral Communication: The ability to express oneself clearly in conversations and interactions with others.

- Speaks clearly and can be easily understood.

- Tailors the content of speech to the level and experience of the audience.

- Uses appropriate grammar and choice of words in oral speech.

- Organizes ideas clearly in oral speech.

- Expresses ideas concisely in oral speech.

- Maintains eye contact when speaking with others.

- Summarizes or paraphrases his understanding of what others have said to verify understanding and prevent miscommunication.

☐ Written Communication: The ability to express oneself clearly in business writing.

- Expresses ideas clearly and concisely in writing.

- Organizes written ideas clearly and signals the organization to the reader.

- Tailors written communications to effectively reach an audience.

- Uses graphics and other aids to clarify complex or technical information.

- Spells correctly.

- Writes using concrete, specific language.

- Uses punctuation correctly.

- Writes grammatically.

- Uses an appropriate business writing style.

☐ Persuasive Communication: The ability to plan and deliver oral and written communications that make an impact and persuade their intended audiences.

- Identifies and presents information or data that will have a strong effect on others.

- Selects language and examples tailored to the level and experience of the audience.

- Selects stories, analogies, or examples to illustrate a point.

- Creates graphics, overheads, or slides that display information clearly and with high impact.

- Presents several different arguments in support of a position.

☐ Interpersonal Awareness: The ability to notice, interpret, and anticipate others' concerns and feelings, and to communicate this awareness empathetically to others.

- Understands the interests and important concerns of others.

- Notices and accurately interprets what others are feeling, based on their choice of words, tone of voice, expressions, and other nonverbal behavior.

- Anticipates how others will react to a situation.

- Listens attentively to people's ideas and concerns.

- Understands both the strengths and the weaknesses of others.

- Understands the unspoken meaning in a situation.

- Says or does things to address others' concerns.

- Finds nonthreatening ways to approach others about sensitive issues.

- Makes others feel comfortable by responding in ways that convey interest in what they have to say.

☐ Influencing Others: The ability to gain others' support for ideas, proposals, projects, and solutions.

- Presents arguments that address others' most important concerns and issues and looks for win-win solutions.

- Involves others in a process or decision to ensure their support.

- Offers trade-offs or exchanges to gain commitment.

- Identifies and proposes solutions that benefit all parties involved in a situation.

- Enlists expert or third parties to influence others.

- Develops other indirect strategies to influence others.

- Knows when to escalate critical issues to management, if own efforts to enlist support have not succeeded.

- Structures situations to create a desired impact and to maximize the chances of a favorable outcome.

- Works to make a particular impression on others.

- Identifies and targets influence efforts at the real decision-makers and those who can influence them.

- Seeks out and builds relationships with others who can provide information, intelligence, career support, potential business, and other forms of help.

- Takes a personal interest in others to develop relationships.

- Accurately anticipates the implications of events or decisions for various stakeholders in the organization, and plans strategy accordingly.

☐ Building Collaborative Relationships: The ability to develop, maintain, and strengthen partnerships with others inside or outside the organization who can provide information, assistance, and support.

- Asks about the other person's personal experiences, interests, and family.

- Asks questions to identify shared interests, experiences, or other common ground.

- Shows an interest in what others have to say; acknowledges their perspectives and ideas.

- Recognizes the business concerns and perspectives of others.

- Expresses gratitude and appreciation to others who have provided information, assistance, or support.

- Takes time to get to know coworkers, to build rapport and establish a common bond.

- Tries to build relationships with people whose assistance, cooperation, and support may be needed.

- Provides assistance, information, and support to others to build a basis for future reciprocity.

☐ Customer Orientation: The ability to demonstrate concern for satisfying one's external and/or internal customers.

- Quickly and effectively solves customer problems.

- Talks to customers to find out what they want and how satisfied they are with what they are getting.

- Lets customers know he is willing to work with them to meet their needs.

- Finds ways to measure and track customer satisfaction.

- Presents a cheerful, positive manner with customers.

II. Competencies Dealing With Business
The Preventing and Solving Problems Cluster

☐ Diagnostic Information Gathering: The ability to identify the information needed to clarify a situation, seek that information from appropriate sources, and use skillful questioning to draw out the information, when others are reluctant to disclose it.

- Identifies the specific information needed to clarify a situation or to make a decision.

- Gets more complete and accurate information by checking multiple sources.

- Probes skillfully to get at the facts, when others are reluctant to provide full, detailed information.

- Routinely walks around to see how people are doing and to hear about any problems they are encountering.

- Questions others to assess whether they have thought through a plan of action.

- Questions others to assess their confidence in solving a problem or tackling a situation.

- Asks questions to clarify a situation.

- Seeks the perspective of everyone involved in a situation.

- Seeks out knowledgeable people to obtain information or clarify a problem.

☐ Analytical Thinking: The ability to tackle a problem by using a logical, systematic, sequential approach.

- Makes a systematic comparison of two or more alternatives.

- Notices discrepancies and inconsistencies in available information.

- Identifies a set of features, parameters, or considerations to take into account in analyzing a situation or making a decision.

- Approaches a complex task or problem by breaking it down into its component parts and considering each part in detail.

- Weighs the costs, benefits, risks, and chances for success in making a decision.

- Identifies many possible causes for a problem.

- Carefully weighs the priority of things to be done.

☐ Forward Thinking: The ability to anticipate the implications and consequences of situations and take appropriate action to be prepared for possible contingencies.

- Anticipates possible problems and develops contingency plans in advance.

- Notices trends in the industry or marketplace and develops plans to prepare for opportunities or problems.

- Anticipates the consequences of situations and plans accordingly.

- Anticipates how individuals and groups will react to situations and information and plans accordingly.

☐ Conceptual Thinking: The ability to find effective solutions by taking a holistic, abstract, or theoretical perspective.

- Notices similarities between different and apparently unrelated situations.

- Quickly identifies the central or underlying issues in a complex situation.

- Creates a graphic diagram showing a systems view of the situation.

- Develops analogies or metaphors to explain a situation.

- Applies a theoretical framework to understand a specific situation.

☐ Strategic Thinking: The ability to analyze the organization's competitive position by considering market and industry trends, existing and potential customers, and strengths and weaknesses as compared to competitors.

- Understands the organization's strengths and weaknesses as compared to competitors.

- Understands industry and market trends affecting the organization's competitiveness.

- Has an in-depth understanding of competitive products and services within the marketplace.

- Develops and proposes a long-term strategy for the organization based on an analysis of the industry and marketplace and the organization's current and potential capabilities as compared to competitors.

☐ Technical Expertise: The ability to demonstrate depth of knowledge and skill in a technical area.

- Effectively applies technical knowledge to solve a range of problems.

- Possesses an in-depth knowledge and skill in a technical area.

- Develops technical solutions to new or highly complex problems that cannot be solved using existing methods or approaches.

- Is sought out as an expert to provide advice or solutions in his technical area.

- Keeps informed about cutting-edge technology in his technical area.

The Achieving Results Cluster

☐ Initiative: Identifying what needs to be done and doing it before being asked or before the situation requires it.

- Identifying what needs to be done and taking action before being asked or the situation requires it.

- Does more than what is normally required in a situation.

- Seeks out others involved in a situation to learn their perspectives.

- Takes independent action to change the direction of events.

☐ Entrepreneurial Orientation: The ability to look for and seize profitable business opportunities; willingness to take calculated risks to achieve business goals.

- Notices and seizes profitable business opportunities.

- Stays abreast of business, industry, and market information that may reveal business opportunities.

- Demonstrates willingness to take calculated risks to achieve business goals.

- Proposes innovative business deals to potential customers, suppliers, and business partners.

- Encourages and supports entrepreneurial behavior in others.

☐ Fostering Innovation: The ability to develop, sponsor, or support the introduction of new and improved methods, products, procedures, or technologies.

- Personally develops a new product or service.

- Personally develops a new method or approach.

- Sponsors the development of new products, services, methods, or procedures.

- Proposes new approaches, methods, or technologies.

- Develops better, faster, or less expensive ways to do things.

- Works cooperatively with others to produce innovative solutions.

☐ Results Orientation: The ability to focus on the desired result of one's own or one's unit's work, setting challenging goals. Focusing effort on the goals, and meeting or exceeding them.

- Develops challenging but achievable goals.

- Develops clear goals for meetings and projects.

- Maintains commitment to goals in the face of obstacles and frustration.

- Finds or creates ways to measure performance against goals.

- Exerts unusual effort over time to achieve a goal.

- Has a strong sense of urgency about solving problems and getting work done.

☐ Thoroughness: Ensuring that one's own work and information are complete and accurate; carefully preparing for meetings and presentations; following up with others to ensure that agreements and commitments have been fulfilled.

- Sets up procedures to ensure high quality of work.

- Monitors the quality of work.

- Verifies information.

- Checks the accuracy of own and other's work.

- Develops and uses systems to organize and keep track of information or work progress.

- Carefully prepares for meetings and presentations.

- Organizes information or material for others.

- Carefully reviews and checks the accuracy of information in work reports provided by management, IT, or other individuals and groups.

☐ Decisiveness: The ability to make decisions in a timely manner.

- Is willing to make decisions in difficult or ambiguous situations, when time is critical.

- Takes charge of a group when it is necessary to facilitate change, overcome an impasse, face issues, or ensure decisions are made.

- Makes tough decisions.

III. Self-Management Competencies

☐ Self-Confidence: Faith in one's own ideas and capability to be successful; willingness to take an independent position in the face of opposition.

- Is confident of own ability to accomplish goals.

- Presents self crisply and impressively.

- Is willing to speak up to the right person or group at the right time, when he disagrees with a decision or strategy.

- Approaches challenging tasks with a "can-do" attitude.

☐ Stress Management: The ability to keep functioning effectively when under pressure and maintain self-control in the face of hostility or provocation.

- Remains calm under stress.

- Can effectively handle several problems or tasks at once.

- Controls his response when criticized, attacked, or provoked.

- Maintains a sense of humor under difficult circumstances.

- Manages own behavior to prevent or reduce feelings of stress.

☐ Personal Credibility: Demonstrated concern that one be perceived as responsible, reliable, and trustworthy.

- Does what he commits to doing.

- Respects the confidentiality of information or concerns shared by others.

- Is honest and forthright with people.

- Carries his fair share of the workload.

- Takes responsibility for own mistakes; does not blame others.

- Conveys a command of the relevant facts and information.

☐ Flexibility: Openness to different and new ways of doing things; willingness to modify one's preferred way of doing things.

- Is able to see the merits of perspectives other than his own.

- Demonstrates openness to new organizational structures, procedures, and technology.

- Switches to a different strategy when an initially selected one is unsuccessful.

- Demonstrates willingness to modify a strongly held position in the face of contrary evidence.

The list of competencies included in this appendix was identified by the authors, Edward J. Cripe and Richard S. Mansfield in their book The Value-Added Employee *published by Butterworth-Heinemann in 2002. The focus is on 31 major competencies along with some behaviors associated with each.*

Reprinted from *The Value-Added Employee—31 Skills to Make Yourself Irresistible to Any Company*, Edward J. Cripe et. al., pp. 134-144, 2001, with perimssion from Elsevier.

Appendix B:
Competencies for
Case Studies

Corporate Attorney

Key Competencies:
- *Achieves Results*
- *Impact and Influence*
- *Customer Service*
- *Analytical Skills*
- *Strategic Agility*
- *Team Orientation*

Questions:

1. Tell me about a time where you used your judgment to persuade a partner or senior manager to make a different decision in a case.

- *Impact and Influence*
- *Customer Service*
- *Team Orientation*
- *Achieves Results*

2. Tell me about a time you used complex litigation analysis in a case. What was the result?

- *Achieves Results*
- *Analytical Skills*

237

3.   Have you used a litigation strategy? Describe a case where you used a litigation strategy to help you manage the case, and tell us the steps you went through to determine the right litigation strategy to use. What happened?

- *Strategic Agility*
- *Analytical Skills*
- *Achieves Results*

4.   Tell us about a time you had to deal with a difficult issue with an employee. How did you handle it? What happened?

- *Impact and Influence*
- *Team Orientation*
- *Customer Service*

5.   Describe a situation where you had to deal with a difficult client. How did you handle the situation?

- *Customer Service*
- *Impact and Influence*
- *Team Orientation*
- *Strategic Agility*

6.   Tell us about a time when you used your skills and knowledge to help the team. What was your role? What was the outcome or result of your input?

- *Team Orientation*
- *Impact and Influence*
- *Achieves Results*

Human Resources Vice President

Key Competencies:

- *Achieves Results*
- *Impact and Influence*
- *Customer Focus*
- *Building Business Partnerships, Relationships, and Teams*
- *Consulting*
- *Organizational Awareness, Agility, and Savvy*
- *Providing Feedback*
- *Understanding Business Goals*
- *Human Resources Expertise*

Questions:

1.   Describe a time that you had to work especially hard to get a good result. What did you do?

- *Achieves Results*
- *Understanding Business Goals*
- *Impact and Influence*
- *Organizational Awareness, Agility, and Savvy*

2.   Tell us about a time that you had to influence a group of people to be able to lead them effectively.

- *Impact and Influence*
- *Building Business Partnerships, Relationships, and Teams*
- *Customer Focus*
- *Achieves Results*
- *Organizational Awareness, Agility, and Savvy*
- *Providing Feedback*

3.   When you first started with your current employer, what did you do to learn the specific things about the industry that you needed to know to be effective in human resources? How did you decide what was especially important?

- *Understanding Business Goals*

- *Customer Focus*

- *Human Resources Expertise*

- *Consulting*

4.   Tell us about one of the most effective business partnerships you've been involved in building. What did you do to help make it so effective? Did you have to overcome any obstacles? Describe what happened.

- *Building Business Partnerships, Relationships, and Teams*

- *Achieves Results*

- *Organizational Awareness, Agility, and Savvy*

- *Impact and Influence*

- *Customer Focus*

- *Providing Feedback*

5.   Have you been involved with introducing any new ideas or programs into your organization? Tell us about the program, and describe the steps you used to improve the acceptance for the program.

- *Understanding Business Goals*

- *Human Resources Expertise*

- *Achieves Results*

- *Impact and Influence*

- *Customer Focus*

- *Building Business Partnerships, Relationships, and Teams*
- *Consulting*
- *Organizational Awareness, Agility, and Savvy*
- *Providing Feedback*

6. Tell us about a time you made a mistake. What did you learn from it?

- *Customer Focus*
- *Building Business Partnerships, Relationships, and Teams*
- *Consulting*
- *Organizational Awareness, Agility, and Savvy*
- *Impact and Influence*

Director, Information Technology

Key Competencies:
- *Creates Innovative Solutions*
- *Thinks Analytically*
- *Acts Strategically and Globally*
- *Drives Results*
- *Exceeds Customer Expectations*
- *Risk-Taking*
- *Acts Decisively*
- *Collaborates and Influences Others*
- *Demonstrates Integrity*
- *Treats People with Respect*
- *Manages Performance*
- *Develops People*
- *Manages Change*

Questions:

1.   Tell us about a situation where you had to take several actions over a period of time and overcome obstacles in order to achieve a business objective.

- *Drives Results*
- *Thinks Analytically*
- *Manages Performance*
- *Acts Strategically and Globally*

2.   Describe a time when you had to identify some key issues in order to guide a group toward the right decision.

- *Collaborates and Influences Others*
- *Thinks Analytically*
- *Acts Strategically and Globally*
- *Drives Results*
- *Acts Decisively*
- *Demonstrates Integrity*
- *Treats People With Respect*
- *Manages Performance*
- *Develops People*

3.   Think of a time when you had many challenging projects with different priorities to manage. Tell us about it.

- *Drives Results*
- *Creates Innovative Solutions*
- *Thinks Analytically*
- *Acts Strategically and Globally*
- *Exceeds Customer Expectations.*
- *Risk-Taking*

- *Acts Decisively*
- *Collaborates and Influences Others*
- *Demonstrates Integrity*
- *Treats People With Respect*
- *Manages Performance*
- *Develops People*
- *Manages Change*

College Graduate, Engineering

Key Competencies
- *Achieved Results*
- *Initiative*
- *Analytical Skills*
- *Customer Service*
- *Engineering and Computer Competencies*
- *Planning and Organizing*
- *Information Seeking*

Questions:

1. Tell me about an assignment in school or at work where you needed to have strong analytical skills to do well. How did you plan and organize the work? How did you decide what information you would need?

- *Analytical Skills*
- *Planning and Organizing*
- *Information Seeking*
- *Initiative*
- *Achieved Results*
- *Technical Competencies*

Appendix C:
Examples of Illegal
Pre-Employment
Interview Questions

1. What is your country of citizenship?

2. When were you born?

3. Where do you go to church?

4. What is your native language?

5. Where were your parents born?

6. Are you married?

7. Do you plan to have children?

8. Are you gay or straight?

9. What are your childcare arrangements?

10. Do you have any disabilities?

11. Have you had any recent illness or operations?

12. What type of military discharge did you obtain?

13. Tell me about your family.

14. When did you graduate from high school?

Notes

Chapter 1

[1] Lou Adler, "The Best Interview Question of All Time." *www.erexchange.com* June 28, 2001.

Chapter 2

[1] *www.ohr.psu.edu/competencies/ohr/Employee %20handbook%20final.pdf*

[2] Adapted from Robert Wood and Tim Payne, *Competency-Based Recruitment and Selection* (Chichester, England: John Wiley & Sons, 1998), 28.

Chapter 3

[1] Source for statistic: *www.eeoc.gov/stats/charges.html*.

Chapter 6

[1] The last seven tips on this list are adapted from De Vito, Joseph A., *Human Communication: The Basic Course*, Fifth Edition (HarperCollins Publishers, 1991), 153.

Chapter 7

[1] Robin Kessler and Linda A. Strasburg, *Competency-Based Resumes: How to Bring Your Resume to the Top of the Pile* (Franklin Lakes, N.J.: Career Press, 2004), 175-177.

Chapter 9

[1] Robin Kessler and Linda A. Strasburg, *Competency-Based Resumes: How to Bring Your Resume to the Top of the Pile* (Franklin Lakes, N.J.: Career Press, 2004), 38.

Chapter 15

[1] Robin Kessler, "Collaborate with Employees to Make Your Competency-Based Systems Stronger." *Employment Relations Today*, Wiley Periodicals, Autumn 2004, 28-30.

Bibliography

Adler, Lou. *Hire With Your Head: Using Power Hiring to Build Great Companies*, Second Edition. Hoboken, N.J.: John Wiley & Sons, Inc., 2002.

Adler, Ronald B., and Jeanne Marquardt Elmhorst. *Communicating at Work: Principles and Practices for Business and the Professions*, 8th edition. Boston: McGraw Hill, 2004.

Boyatzis, Richard. *The Competent Manager: A Model for Effective Performance*. New York: John Wiley and Sons, 1982.

Cooper, Kenneth Carlton. *Effective Competency Modeling and Reporting: A Step-by-Step Guide for Improving Individual & Organizational Performance*. New York: Amacom, 2000.

Cripe, Edward J., and Richard S. Mansfield. *The Value-Added Employee*. Woodburn, Mass.: Butterworth-Heinemann, 2002.

DeVito, Joseph. *Human Communication: The Basic Course*, 9th edition. Boston: Allyn & Bacon, 2002.

Dobkin, Bethami, and Roger C. Pace. *Communication in a Changing World*. Boston: McGraw Hill, 2003.

Fry, Ron. *101 Great Answers to the Toughest Interview Questions*, Third Edition. Franklin Lakes, N.J.: Career Press, 1996.

Green, Paul C. *Building Robust Competencies: Linking Human Resources Systems to Organizational Strategies*. San Francisco: Jossey-Bass, 1999.

Kessler, Robin, and Linda A. Strasburg. *Competency-Based Resumes: How to Bring Your Resume to the Top of the Pile*. Franklin Lakes, N.J.: Career Press, 2004.

Lombardo, Michael M., and Robert W. Eichinger. *The Leadership Machine: Architecture to Develop Leaders for Any Future*. Minneapolis: Lominger, 2001.

Powers, Dr. Paul. *Winning Job Interviews: Reduce Interview Anxiety / Outprepare the Other Candidates/Land the Job You Love*. Franklin Lakes, N.J.: Career Press, 2004.

Quinn, Carol. *Don't Hire Anyone Without Me!: A Revolutionary Approach to Interviewing & Hiring the Best*. Franklin Lakes, N.J.: Career Press, 2001.

Spencer, Jr., Lyle M., PhD, and Signe M. Spencer. *Competence at Work: Models for Superior Performance*. New York: John Wiley & Sons, Inc., 1993.

Wendleton, Kate. *Interviewing and Salary Negotiation*. Clifton Park, N.Y.: Thomson Delmar Learning, 1999.

——. *Mastering the Job Interview and Winning the Money Game*. Clifton Park, N.Y.: Thomson Delmar Learning, 2005.

Wood, Robert, and Tim Payne. *Competency-Based Recruitment and Selection: A Practical Guide*. Chichester, England: John Wiley & Sons, 2003.

Yates, Martin. *Knock 'Em Dead 2005: The Ultimate Job Seekers Guide*. Avon, Mass.: Adams Media Corporation, 2004.

Index

About the Author

Robin Kessler is president of The Interview Coach, a human resources and career consulting firm based in Houston; she also teaches *Business and Professional Communication* and *Interviewing Skills* as an adjunct professor for the University of Houston–Downtown. Robin has more than 20 years of experience improving interviews, resumes, presentations, and organization communication as a human resources professional, consultant, and career coach. She was the lead author for the book *Competency-Based Resumes: How to Bring Your Resume to the Top of the Pile*, published by Career Press in November 2004. She has written articles on current issues in organization communication and speaking skills for publications including *HR Magazine*, *Employment Relations Today*, and the *Houston Chronicle*; has been a guest speaker at conferences; and has been interviewed for newspapers, magazines, and radio and television programs. Robin received her B.A. and M.B.A. (M.M.) from Northwestern University. Please contact her with your comments at *intvcoach@aol.com*.